JOHNNY APPLESEED

in a Rich Land

by

Peggy Welch Mershon

No part of this publication may be reproduced or transmitted in any form or by any means, electronic or technical, including photocopying, recording, or by any information storage or retrieval system, without permission in writing from the publisher.

© 2019 by Peggy Welch Mershon.
All Rights Reserved.

Photo Credits:
Robert A. Carter, Figure 5; Mansfield Bicentennial Committee, Figure 8; H. C Knapp, *History of Ashland County*, 1862: Figure 21; E. Bonar McLaughlin, M.D., *Pioneer History and Scrap Book*, 1887: Figure 22.

Johnny Appleseed in a Rich Land

by

Peggy Welch Mershon

ISBN-13: 978-0-9982215-9-5

www.TurasPublishing.com

To the late historian and author ***Dwight Wesley Garber*** and his fascination not only with John Chapman but also with the people of Richland County, Ohio, who recorded the real person, as they remembered him.

Worship does not consist in prayers and in external devotion, but in a life of kindness.

~ Emanuel Swedenborg

Table of Contents

List of Figures vii

Introduction 1

Chapter One • *Emanuel Swedenborg: John Chapman's Faith* . 7

Chapter Two • *A Rare Find by Historian D. W. Garber* 13

Chapter Three • *The First of the Authors* 22

Chapter Four • *The War of 1812* 28

Chapter Five • *The Massacre* 33

Chapter Six • *The Battle* 57

Chapter Seven • *Salathiel* 84

Chapter Eight • *History Finally Recognized and Recorded* . . 93

Chapter Nine • *A Glorified Pioneer History* 104

Chapter Ten • *Rosella Rice Stories* 109

Chapter Eleven • *More Rosella Rice Stories* 124

Chapter Twelve • *Dr. William Bushnell* 148

Chapter Thirteen • *Horace S. Knapp's Frontispiece* 157

Afterword 163

Acknowledgments (Author) 165

Acknowledgments (D. W. Garber) 171

The Author Peggy Welch Mershon 175

List of Figures

Figure		Page
1.	Emanuel Swedenborg.	8
2.	The Cover of Wessen's Catalog, Number 30	14
3.	The Page with Details about Item 246	15
4.	The Page with an Illustration of Item 246	16
5.	Historian D.W. Garber	17
6.	Ernest Wessen	18
7.	Salathiel Coffinberry	23
8.	Coffinberry Cabin	24
9.	Wright Coffinberry	25
10.	"The Massacre"	34
11.	"The Battle"	59
12.	Roeliff Brinkerhoff	94
13.	Rosella Rice	109
14.	Alexander Rice	110
15.	Nathaniel Chapman Letter	119
16.	Nathaniel Chapman (continued)	121
17.	Rosella Manuscript	125
18.	Appleseed Receipt	146
19.	Dr. William Bushnell	148
20.	Johnny Appleseed Monument	149
21.	Honorable M. H. Bushnell	150
22.	Horace S. Knapp's Frontiespiece	158
23.	Sketch of Johnny Appleseed with Different Hat	159

Introduction

John Chapman was born in Leominster, Massachusetts, on September 26, 1774, and died in Fort Wayne, Indiana, on March 18, 1845. For many of the years in the middle, some say as many as 30, he used Richland County, Ohio, as his base. He lived there, he planted apple seeds and medicinal plants there, he sold seedlings for orchards there, and he was determined to spread the word of his deeply held Swedenborgian religion there.

Even though at times he wandered without fanfare north to Lake Erie or south to his family near the Ohio River, he and most of the people of Richland County considered themselves neighbors and friends. The testimony of these early settlers is vital in assessing the character and characteristics of the man who was eventually known as Johnny Appleseed.

Many books about this iconic American figure written over the years carefully count what could be proven about his life—how many apple nurseries were planted, how many acres bought and sold, who was owed what—but practically all the personal testimony has been reduced in importance. No written records, no proven truth, the historians maintained.

Starting with *Johnny Appleseed: Man and Myth* by Robert Price of Ohio's Otterbein College in 1954, anything official involving John Chapman from his birth, land records, and apple seedling sales has been scrupulously dug out and recorded. These facts are crucial for they prove the man was real and establish where he lived. But also important is the recording and printing of the stories he evoked in the one place he called home the longest—Richland County, Ohio.

Legends swirling around John Chapman are legion and often exaggerated and warped through the years in various places from various people. Often the original source was from Richland County where he was well known. Those original stories, from people who actually knew him, need to be uncovered and recorded. Some may be obviously fictional but others may hold a golden kernel of truth. We need to read them in order to judge.

Learning about John Chapman's life from his own words would be ideal, but unfortunately, while others presented him as quite literate and very talkative, almost none of his letters or—can it be hoped?—journals were preserved. If he did write letters, his family and friends apparently threw them away. He preferred to talk about his religious beliefs rather than to write about them. He left the writing to others. Instead he carried printed tracts of the actual words of Emanuel Swedenborg tucked into his shirt.

It would have been highly unusual for a man who spent so much time traipsing through the frontier woods on foot to maintain a safe place for keeping written correspondence and records. These records may have existed once, but as far as anyone can determine, they do not exist today. Letters were mentioned, mainly by the Swedenborgian church, but apparently none were preserved. A few signed business notes, dashed off in his neat handwriting, have been found in Richland, saved by families as evidence of what was owed by him or to him.

Mostly what was saved were the memories of people who knew him directly and who were persuaded to write those memories down while still fresh—people who welcomed him into their cabins and held long conversations, mostly about his religion. He also injected himself, according to those memories, into their lives, happy over their newborns and delighted to jiggle toddlers on his knee. He gossiped with the best of them, spreading his own facts, rumors, and warnings. Telling tales, even ruthlessly based on facts, was a source of entertainment among the settlers. He may have traveled alone in the woods and knew the pathways, but he was no hermit.

Richland County is fortunate to have had a number of skillful early storytellers. Their written accounts of the odd but beloved John Chapman have been resurrected, often from oblivion, and included here.

Richland County originally was one of the largest counties in the new state of Ohio—about 30 miles square when the first three surveyors began carving it up into sections in 1806. James Hedges and Jacob Newman, two of the earliest settlers, platted the town in 1808 that eventually became the county seat—Mansfield.

Richland County was first placed under the governmental jurisdiction of Knox County, adjacent to the south, until 1813 when it stood on its own. The boundaries of the county were shaved off over the years, mostly in the 1840s, until today when it is roughly 500 square miles. Townships came and went from county to county. This included the creation in 1846 of what is now Ashland County to the east. Johnny Appleseed was particularly fond of this area, with its town of Perrysville, and at times he lived there in an old log cabin on the Rice family property.

He moved away to Indiana when Ohio's population grew and the boundaries began changing. Perhaps he first came to the area of Richland County because the soil was rich, thus the name, and the water gushed freely from the Mohican River and its tributaries. It was a great place for seedlings and for future settlement, his main concerns.

Most of his biographies say he and perhaps his oldest half brother, Nathaniel, arrived in Ohio as early as 1801, crossing the river to Jefferson County. He traveled with his load of Pennsylvania apple seeds down the Ohio rivers, often in double canoes, aiming for land not yet settled and awaiting the earliest pioneers to plant its orchards.

Unlike what simplified fables later indicated, Chapman did not just scatter seeds. He was said to always plant and tend his seeds carefully so they not only supplied settlers with nourishment but with the legal requirements, in the form of orchards, to hold claims to land. He also spread certain medicinal herbs so that the pioneers would have remedies close to their cabins. This seems to indicate he was mostly concerned, as his religion directed, about the well-being of the settlers.

In 1805, he and Nathaniel brought their father, also Nathaniel; his second wife, Lucy Cooley; and their young brood of children to settle near Marietta, Ohio. There, many of their descendants would stay, but a half sister, Persis, 19 years younger, married William Broom and moved to Richland County with their daughters. Eventually they moved with Johnny to about 40 miles from Fort Wayne. While he may have depended on them for help with businesses, they, from local stories, also depended on him for economic survival.

Evidence shows that he maintained amiable contact with his real family in Ohio, although none appeared to be overly enchanted by his growing reputation. It was said, without evidence, that he helped bury his father in 1807 and that he often visited half brothers and sisters. Tales of his roaming the Ohio woods alone might very well have been his trips to see family and friends.

The first official record that a John Chapman was in the neighborhood of Richland County came with his purchase of two town lots in Knox County's Mount Vernon in 1809. It is quite possible that he also wandered northward, and Richland County pioneers later claimed that his plantings of apple seedlings, and perhaps even Chapman himself, were waiting for them when they began to arrive around 1808. Although there are no records in either county, only the stories of him planting his seeds in places likely to benefit early settlers remain.

In fact, the settlers would not document buying Johnny Appleseed seedlings and moving them to their own property until at least a decade later. By the time he left for Indiana in the 1840s, people were eager to claim every orchard came originally from his seedlings, no matter how often they grafted the buds themselves. Others soon followed him in planting apples, but settlers seemed to appreciate Johnny's way of doing things.

Despite his many oddities—he was far from the typical settler with a typical family—John Chapman was useful, sometimes pleasantly so. He planted welcome, inexpensive, apple seeds and nurtured them to saleable seedlings; he even spread weeds he deemed useful for health; he brought useful messages and information—what dangers may lurk, whose baby had its first tooth—and he spoke well about his own beliefs (sometimes this was less than useful for Methodists from Maryland). He was interesting and not demanding of others to take care of him. He took care of others. He was helpful to the settlers and most liked him for it. He thought this was his religious role, his constant, deliberate intention. Do no harm, only good, was his aim, and people saw that they benefited from that.

Many pioneers of Richland County were still alive with varying degrees of memories when he packed up, with his half sister and her family, for Indiana, which was just a little wilder, a little less settled by the white man, and a little more needy of his apples and his words. Up to his death there in 1845, he was recorded as coming back to Richland County to pay taxes, to check progress, and to visit friends. Then he faded away, and many were not sure when they last saw him, but they remembered those earlier years.

This is a book primarily of those memories, which others may have ignored. For those who prefer a brick-and-mortor recitation of his life, from before birth to after death, I suggest Robert Price's book. It has never been out of print. Many subsequent biographies have appeared, often borrowing heavily and sometime incorrectly from what was published before. Some are better than others. Read those too, selectively.

Price was the first history professional studying Chapman's life who spent years traveling around the state searching for evidence, and finding, often for the first time, provable bits and pieces of John Chapman's frontier life. He also picked up what he considered was interesting but less useful—what he labeled myth—but what also included testimonials and pioneer stories.

What he did provided an invaluable base for further research; but, out of necessity, he was a fleeting stranger to specific places. He failed to discover two of those stories that appeared in a Mansfield newspaper, the *Richland Jeffersonian*, in 1839 and 1840 when Johnny Appleseed was alive and dividing his time between Richland County and Indiana. Johnny may have even read them and chuckled.

These stories survive today only because of the sharp eye of Richland County historian Dwight Wesley Garber, born in 1896 to pioneer families. Here is, first, Garber's story of discovery and then the early newspaper stories written by another man who as a baby arrived in Mansfield, at its own birth, in 1808, a man who knew John Chapman all his life.

Today, practically everything involving Johnny Appleseed is about apples. Apples are easier to understand than the religion he was promoting. But in the beginning of the stories about the mysterious missionary, everyone knew him first as a Swedenborgian, and many were happy to sit down and discuss it with him. He did not make a lot of converts, but the religion's tenants, Johnny's particular interpretation and devotion to them —and apples—made him a good and welcome neighbor.

Peggy Welch Mershon

Chapter One

Emanuel Swedenborg: John Chapman's Faith

When John Chapman first entered Ohio around 1801, he brought not only bags of apple seeds but also a belief in the philosophy of the Swedish scientist and theologian Emanuel Swedenborg. Whether or not he arrived with the intent of telling everyone he met about the Church of the New Jerusalem, he ended up doing exactly that.

Because this philosophy played such a large part in Chapman's life and his interaction with the people around him, a short summary of the Church of the New Jerusalem and of those in Richland County who were moved to share Chapman's way of thinking is presented here.

Swedenborg (1688-1772) preceded Chapman by quite a few years, but his was a rather new way of thought to Americans at the end of the 18th century. Chapman was first drawn to these teachings when traveling through Pennsylvania in his twenties. The New Church lecturers began arriving in 1784, and reading groups began popping up on the East Coast about five years later.

It was a rather complex, intellectual religion, although Swedenborg had no intention of turning it into an actual Christian church with hierarchy and rituals. According to his biography, the scientist became a theologian rather late in his life (1744), complete with dreams and revelations.

Figure 1. Emanuel Swedenborg.

He wrote at least 18 books, believed divinely inspired, and indeed he thought he talked directly to God and others who had already "crossed over." He believed heaven and hell existed on Earth, and that it was everyone's duty to unselfishly serve his fellow man. Salvation, and therefore eternal peace, was earned only by good works. Poverty was better than wealth, self-denial better than self-promotion. A person was only as good in heaven, or as bad in hell, as they were on Earth. Chapman respected life on Earth, down to snakes and insects, because they existed simultaneously in the spirit world.

This new religion required not only intellect but also much studying, ideal for a man who spent many hours alone in the woods. For some reason this appealed to Chapman, although there is no evidence anyone else in his family was sympathetic. It may have been his motivation for going to Ohio since a follower, William Grant, had crossed the river to spread the word in Steubenville, Jefferson County, about 1797. Chapman followed with sacks of apple seeds in 1800 or 1801. He was probably carrying Swedenborgian pamphlets (referred to as tracts,) even then in his shirt.

The Swedenborg organization is credited with the first printed mention of Chapman, and although he was not referred to by name, it was obvious that it was him. The Manchester, England, Society for Printing, Publishing and Circulating the Writings of

Emanuel Swedenborg on January 14, 1817, learned of Chapman's continually turning income from apple seedlings into book orders when it wrote:

> There is in the western country a very extraordinary missionary of the New Jerusalem. A man has appeared who seems to be almost independent of corporeal wants and sufferings. He goes barefoot, and sleeps anywhere, in house or out of house, and lives upon the coarsest and most scanty fare. He actually thawed the ice with bare feet.

Amazingly, clear over in England, this sounds very much like what Richland County settlers were saying among themselves. It no doubt came from here in "the western country."

The society continued:

> He procures what books he can of the New Church, travels to remote settlements and lends them wherever he can find readers, and sometimes divides a book into two or three parts for more extensive distribution and usefulness. The man for years past has been in the employment of bringing into cultivation, in numerous places in the wilderness, small patches (two or three acres) of ground, and then sowing apple seeds and rearing nurseries.
>
> These become valuable as the settlements approximate, and the profits of a whole are intended for the purpose of enabling him to print all the writings of Emanuel Swedenborg, and distribute them through the western settlements of the United States.

The faith spread sparsely but quickly, limited in some degree, by how hard it was to understand, and accept, and by the hostility of the more traditional frontier religions, like Evangelical Lutheranism and Methodism. John Chapman did not preach in the usual way, standing before congregations and collecting herds of converts, but rather he conversed and explained in the log cabin, hoping the tracts and his interpretation would encourage an understanding.

The first reference to John Chapman by name was in 1822 in the New Jerusalem journal of the fifth convention in Philadelphia:

> Besides the society established at Steubenville...and Lebanon and the very numerous church of Cincinnati... one very extraordinary missionary continues to exert, for the spread of divine truth, his modest and humble efforts, which would put the most zealous members to the blush. We now allude to Mr. J. Chapman, from whom we are in the habit of hearing frequently. His temporal employment consists in preceding the settlements, and sowing nurseries of fruit trees, which he avows to be pursued for the chief purpose of giving him an opportunity of spreading the Doctrines throughout the western country. In his progress, which neither heat nor cold, swamps nor mountains, are permitted to arrest, he carries on his back all the New Church publications he can procure, and distributes them wherever opportunity is afforded. So great is his zeal, that he does not hesitate to divide his volumes into parts, and, by repeated calls, enable the readers to peruse the whole in succession. Having no family, and inured to hardships of every kind, his operations are unceasing. He is now employed in traversing the district between Detroit and the closer settlements of Ohio. What shall be the reward of such an individual, where, as we are told in the Holy Writ, "They that turn many to righteousness shall shine as the stars forever."

Considering how often John Chapman reportedly wrote letters and ordered books from the Swedenborgians, one would think some, somewhere, would have survived, but no such luck. Letters, written by others and mentioning Chapman, were passed among members of the church. Some of these were saved. As for their letters to him, he probably picked up his mail at various post offices, but he certainly did not seem to keep them.

One of the former in fact was waved around Mansfield and appeared in the newspaper on November 23, 1958, by rare-book seller Ernest Wessen, who thought Chapman was overrated as a historical figure. However, he did view the letter as proof that Chapman lived here in 1821. This proof was hardly necessary, but the letter, dated May 15, 1821, was written by Daniel Thunn, a Philadelphia bookseller and printer specializing in Swedenborgian publications, to Margaret Bailey, one of the founders of the Cincinnati church.

Wessen purchased the letter, according to the *News Journal* article, along with other papers from a Bailey descendent in Dayton. It reads, in part:

> To add something more to the New Church, there is a Mr. John Chapman near Wooster, O., who wrote lately to Mr. Schlatter [William Schlatter, a sponsor of the Swedenborgian society in Philadelphia] that he found an increase of Receivers all around his neighborhood and that they are spreading as far as Detroit, he proposed to make a Deed over to the New Church for a Quarter Section of Land and take payment in books of the New Church. We contemplate how best to fulfill his wishes. This is the Appleseed man you certainly must have heard of, who goes around in the country to plant apple trees.

The "transfer of land" never happened, but Wessen was proud that he had a letter that was authentic evidence and overrode all the word-of-mouth stories that had been floating around Mansfield since 1809. But it was not "new data," as the headline indicated. The letter had been reprinted before, in several books, and Wessen did not say to whom he sold it. What it did show was that Chapman was in continual contact with various Swedenborgian followers.

His signature appears on a petition for the ordination of a Silas Ensign. Formerly a Methodist, Ensign and his new congregation built a church in 1822 near North Woodbury, then in Richland County, now in Morrow County. The church burned about 1827, and Ensign, and probably his congregation, returned to Methodism.

Several other congregations existed around Richland County; there is some evidence that Chapman had influenced their members. John Tucker, the head of a church in Hastings, Monroe Township, said in an 1880 county history he owed a lot to the inspiration of Chapman. In addition, Henry Weirich led a congregation in Petersburgh, now Mifflin, and J.M. Ozier in Olivesburg. By 1844, according to the *New Jerusalem Magazine*, 41 societies were established all over Ohio.

The Swedenborgians seemed to claim and embrace John Chapman from the beginning, as did he them. Besides many books and references to him in its literature, there is a Johnny Appleseed Educational Center and Museum opened in 2011 at the university founded by them in Urbana, Ohio. References to the religion followed him and often defined him from his first days here.

Chapter Two

A Rare Find by Historian D. W. Garber

John Chapman was called not Johnny Appleseed but "the Swedenberger" in the first printed story about him that appeared in Mansfield's *Richland Jeffersonian* on December 28, 1839. Followed by another on March 28 and April 4, 1840, these are the first known accounts in which this legendary figure was intertwined as the hero. Two men in Mansfield, for two quite different reasons, saved these issues, and today they are still the only copies known to exist.

These exceedingly rare printed accounts of John Chapman were discovered in 1946 in two original issues of the weekly newspaper *Richland Jeffersonian*, also exceedingly rare. Few issues, except those mostly with later dates, are found anywhere, including Mansfield. They were published during Chapman's life—he may have read them—by an author who knew him. Any truth they contain must be evaluated based on that fact.

Whatever the motivation may have been behind the unusual, although recognizable name, "the Swedenberger," that same thinking gave all the characters, who were quite real, thinly veiled names. Readers of this local newspaper almost certainly knew who all the characters were supposed to be. Perhaps the names were used in print as a courtesy or it may have been common practice at the time.

In 1946, the content of these *Richland Jeffersonion* newspapers had been forgotten, but these two issues, March 28 and April 4, 1840, fell into the hands of a nationally respected book and paper seller who also called Mansfield home, Ernest J. Wessen.

Figure 2. The Cover of Wessen's Catalog, Number 30.

238. Rerick, Rowland H. History of Ohio. Covering the periods of Indian, French and British Dominion, the Territory Northwest of the Ohio, and the hundred years of Statehood. 10 by 6 5/8 inches, 406p, 3/4 leather, Madison Wis. 1905 $5.00

RICHLAND COUNTY

239. Imperial ATLAS and Art Folio of Richland County Ohio. 19 3/8 by 16 3/8 inches, 67p and map, sloth, Richmond, Ind. 1896 $15.00

240. RICHLAND AND CRAWFORD COUNTIES..ART WORK OF. Published in twelve parts. 13 3/4 by 10 3/4 inches, 12 original parts in wrappers, unpaged, Chicago, 1894 $10.00

241. BAUGHMAN, A. J. Centennial Biographical History of Richland County, Ohio. 10½ by 7½ inches, 696p, morroco, Chicago, 1901 $8.50

242. BAUGHMAN, A. J. History of Richland County from 1808 to 1908, also biographical sketches of prominent citizens. Two volumes, 10 by 7 inches, 1175 & V p, Chicago, 1908 $12.50

243. GRAHAM A. A. History of Richland County, Ohio. 9 3/4 by 7½ inches, 941p, cloth, Mansfield, Ohio, 1880 $12.50

244. M'GAW, REV. JAMES F. Philip Seymour, or Pioneer Life in Richland County, Ohio. Founded on Facts. 8 by 5 inches, 295p, cloth, Mansfield, 1858 $50.00
   By far the finest copy we know of. Thomson 753. Perhaps Thomson's greatest weakness was his tendency to appraise a book without taking the trouble to investigate. In his day a few letters would have produced the truth concerning such narratives as Edward's OHIO HUNTER; the BRAYTON NARRATIVE, and PHILIP SEYMOUR. For Edwards was alive and viogorous in Thomson's day; many who knew Brayton, the Captive, were alive, and many who knew the facts concerning M'Gaw's work on Philip Seymour. In commenting upon the present work he his guilty of a curious boner: "Many historical facts throwing light upon the transactions related in "Philip Seymour" will be found in Knapps' History of Ashland County." Had Thomson given Knapp more than a cursory examination he would have noted that Knapp gave M'Gaw full credit as the source for the light thrown upon those "transactions."
   It is true that was in possession of a "skeleton of facts" as will be seen below; it is equally true that he did a great deal of local research in connection with "Johnny Appleseed", and incidents in pioneer life. His fictional treatment of the Copus Massacre will stand as the most authentic source. For the basic source see No. 246.

245. M'Gaw, Rev. James F. Philip Seymour; or, Pioneer Life in Richland County, Ohio. Founded on Facts. Second edition. 8 1/8 by 5½ inches, 432p cloth, Mansfield, Ohio, 1883. $7.50
   The best edition for general use; in that the publisher, Roeliff Brinkerhoff provides a biographical account of M'Gaw; Rosella Rice provides a first-hand account of Johnny Appleseed from her recolledtions of him, and also present are the proceedings at the erection of the Monument on the site of the massacre.

THE SKELETON OF FACTS

246. THE RICHLAND JEFFERSONIAN, Mansfield, Ohio, March 28 and April 4, 1840. Thomson, in his reference to Philip Seymour refers to a skeleton of facts in M'Gaw's possession. We have discovered and herewith bring that

Figure 3. The page with details about Item 246 at the bottom.

> **THE BATTLE.**
> *A Tale connected with the first settlement of Mansfield, by Gottfried, Author of Scenes at Melsfield, Una-te-was-ka The Massacre, &c. &c.*
>
> **CHAPTER I.**
> "A simple tale, and little worth, save that 'twas owre true!" SCOTCH TALES.
>
> Yet bore he such a dauntless mein,
> It seemed to mock at Fate, until she tired
> Of her own importance.———————"
> *"Anon.*
>
> After the massacre of the Seymore family, it may well be supposed, that consternation, and fears seized the settlers on the line of frontier; the same apprehensions which caused a shudder of horror to thrill through the bosoms of the villagers of Mansfield, reached as far south as Clinton and Mount Vernon, and then had no less appalling an effect. Repeatedly was Copus warned by the villagers, of the dangers to which he exposed himself and family, by remaining at his settlement on the Black Fork, but all in vain; he persisted to remain in his little cabin, with no other means of defence than that afforded by a couple of rifles, with no other hands to wield them, or eyes to direct them but his own, and those of his tw...
> The idea, at this d...

No. 246

skeleton from its closet. In his account of M'Gaw, and his work on PHILIP SEYMOUR, Roeliff Brinkerhoff makes no mention of the RICHLAND JEFFERSONIAN. As a matter of fact Brinkerhoff bought the JEFFERSONIAN; of which these two unique numbers have just come into our possession. Therein, 18 years before the appearance of M'Gaw's work; appears the fictionalized account of the COPUS HILL MASSACRE (See illustration above)...the "skeleton of facts"; which M'Gaw adopted, lock-stock-and-barrel, and following the same style of treatment, expanded with the facts produced by his independent investigations.   SOLD

Also See HISTORY OF NORTH CENTRAL OHIO, No. 211.

247. St Clair, Major General Arthur. A Narrative of the manner in which the Campaign against the Indians, in the year One Thousand Seven Hundred and Ninety One was conducted, etc. $8\frac{1}{4}$ by 5 1/8 inches, 273p, frontispiece, leather, PHILADELPHIA, 1812. $15.00
  Thomson 1012. Fine copy with both lists of subscribers. A tiny piece clipped from upper corner of titlepage. Laid in is an account of the sale of St Clair's papers.

248. ST CLAIR PAPERS. The Life and Public Services of Arthur St Clair, * * *with his Correspondence and other Papers. Arranged and annotated by William Henry Smith. Two volumes, 9 by 6 inches, 609 and 649p, original cloth, Cincinnati, 1882.   Fine set $6.50

Figure 4. The page with an illustration of Item 246.

Dwight Wesley (D.W.) Garber snapped them up for $7.50 on October 11, 1946, according to his later notes, along with a slew of Clinton (a town in Knox County now defunct) *Ohio Registers* from 1813 and 1814, even before they all appeared in Wessen's popular catalog (No. 30), all listed as "sold." Garber no doubt had an advance peek, although Wessen never let his customers know publicly where he found some pretty impressive material—bad business.

When Garber retired from the Navy in 1945, he returned with his wife Vera and his daughter Connie to the place of his birth, Richland County, where his ancestors had been living for six generations. Always interested in history, when growing up in the small town of Butler he poked his nose in numerous tales of long ago, many times gathering information from older relatives, as well as collecting and preserving testimony and evidence.

Figure 5. Historian D.W. Garber.

A complete account of his life and work appears in the book, *Water-Powered Mills of Richland County*, Turas Publishing, 2015, by his friend and long-time history associate, Robert A. Carter of Mansfield, and by Garber's grandson, Michael C. Cullen.

Once back in Richland County, Garber jumped into continuing local historical research, sometimes giving Wessen a run for his money. He wrote 176 weekly newspaper columns for the *Mansfield News Journal;* he published a number of other books, some for the Ohio Historical Society (OHS); and he sold articles to other newspapers and publications. He became an expert on such ranging topics as grain mills, the explorer

Jedediah Strong Smith, Mormons, and wildcat frontier banks. He was always thrilled when finding new historical information through local sources.

It was natural then that he quickly found Wessen. Garber even worked as a book scout for Wessen until one conversation offended the bookseller and ended their friendship. Both were direct, opinionated men.

Figure 6. Ernest Wessen.

Garber later claimed the *Richland Jeffersonians* sat on his shelf, unread, for two years until he finally saw that they contained on their front pages, the articles by an anonymous writer named "Gottfried" that featured, for the first time, John Chapman as a leading character in local history.

It could be argued that the story was fictionalized because it was very conversational, did not follow history closely, and mixed characters at will. It, however, was very entertaining and told about a War of 1812 attack well known to the readers.

In the 1940s, Garber was delighted, not only with his discovery, but also that Wessen "didn't know what he had." Until Wessen died in the 1970s, the pursuer of history considered Johnny taking up too much space in local stories and had a long list of more acceptable local figures.

Wessen did have a much different viewpoint than Garber on the papers' value. He presented them not so much for Johnny Appleseed content but rather as evidence of a "skeleton" for the popular local 1857 novel, *Philip Seymour, or Pioneer Life in Richland County* by James McGaw. Wessen got that skeleton description from an earlier bibliophile, Peter Gibson Thomas, who had written a listing of Ohio books in 1880, so it was no secret, at least then.

As late as 1962, the newly published *Ohio Authors and their Books* had added, under the *Philip Seymour* listing, most likely with help from Wessen, that these *Richland Jeffersonians* had been the direct predecessor of the *Mansfield Herald*, where McGaw worked collecting and writing history. When they were found in the files, it was presumed they were the skeleton where he hung pioneer remembrances.

The 1840 issues of the *Richland Jeffersonian* contained Gottfried's article "The Battle" about the 1812 Indian attack on the Copus cabin, which was about eight miles, as the crow flies, from Mansfield. There is no doubt, from various contemporaneous sources, that the fatal attack happened; but the details, including who were there, changed often over the years, even among the survivors.

Somehow, Garber also found another scarce *Jeffersonian*, a December 28, 1839, issue which contained the first half of another article, "The Massacre" by Gottfried—an account of another attack by Indians a few days before on the Zeimer (or Zimmer or Seymour) cabin not far from the Copus cabin. It also contains details on "the Swedenberger." Garber may have bought this issue, unadvertised, from Wessen, or he may have found it in the files at the Western Reserve Historical Museum in Cleveland, where a copy exists today. He never said. The second half of the story has not been found.

The two 1840 *Jeffersonians* that Garber bought from Wessen are now (2019) at Western Reserve as well, and friends definitely remember that he donated them. Librarians there now say no record exists of who donated them or when they were donated, and according to them, the newspapers are not in very good condition. How unfortunate, as these 1839 and 1840 issues are the only ones that have been found despite a lot of searching by Garber and myself. Whatever later issues exist, they do not have anything about Johnny Appleseed or by Gottfried in them.

But back in the 1940s, eventually reading those *Jeffersonians* sent Garber on many years of research for a book on Johnny

Appleseed that would properly frame his wonderful find of the first known fictionalized story about him. He was almost obsessively dedicated to the task, and the book would develop into the numerous ways the people of Richland County turned the curious but beloved John Chapman into Johnny Appleseed over the 30 years he lived among them.

Garber was convinced that Richland County and its people, whom he well knew, played a big part in the story of Johnny Appleseed, although the editors at the Ohio Historical Society were not convinced that such unknowns should take so much space, according to Garber's correspondence with them. After years of research and uncovering material, Garber spent 1968 through 1972 revising his manuscript to their specifications.

The society seemed to think the highly regarded book on Johnny Appleseed by professional historian Robert Price of Otterbein College, published in 1954, as the target to shoot for, and they even consulted Price about Garber's manuscript. He was kind but hesitant about the approach. Editors hinted they wanted a book with new information, corrected information even, especially considering Garber's talent for finding local details. Despite many years of research and his academic qualifications, Price did not live in Richland County, and he did not know the area as Garber did.

Editors quite literally wanted Johnny Appleseed's name on every page. In other words, they did not want a book they were sure would only interest "local readers," despite the fact that Johnny Appleseed called Richland County home for so long, and these actually were interesting people. Even though nothing that John Chapman wrote, outside of bills, survived, the memories of his neighbors did, but the editors were not enthusiastic about that. They seemed to agree with Price that much was only "folk memories," never mind that they were informative and entertaining.

Despite the friendship and respect that existed between Garber and OHS based on earlier publications and his willingness to revise, revise, revise, this Johnny Appleseed book was never quite what OHS wanted, and it was never published. Eventually, OHS financial problems played a part in the historical society's ability to fund the project.

So D.W. Garber marketed the book, unsuccessfully, to other publishers. When he and his wife moved to California in 1970 to be near their daughter, other projects caught his interest and expertise. He died there at age 87 in 1984, leaving behind a lot of unpublished research on a variety of subjects. Much of his painstaking work is included here, especially his startling discovery of the 1840 stories as well as his determined and exhausting hunt for both the published and unpublished writings of pertinent Richland County authors.

Research in the years before computers was much different than it is today, requiring travels to the library, the courthouse, and to visit people who still had treasures rotting away in chicken coops. It required talking to many people who are no longer alive today. Garber's interest insured that a lot of this material survived, both original and copied. Who knows how much history has been destroyed over the years, including newspapers like the *Richland Jeffersonian*, by disinterested or careless people?

Garber's own acknowledgments of the people, many Richland Countians, who helped his research appears at the end of this book. The three rare *Richland Jeffersonian* articles appear here in print for the first time since 1840.

Chapter Three

The First of the Authors

On Saturday, December 28, 1839, a full-page, page-one story appeared in a Mansfield weekly newspaper, the *Richland Jeffersonian*. Its title, "The Massacre," was enticing. Written by Gottfried, a pen name, the author was also credited with other works, "Scenes at Medfield," "Indian Punishment," "Un-Tee-Was-Ka," etc., suggesting the reader should have been familiar with him. Also on the page was a long poem, also by Gottfried, "The Flower of Mortality," dealing with lots of references to flowers and with nature's treatment of fleeting glory.

Only the first part of the story appears in this issue, to be continued the next week and maybe even those following. Unfortunately those newspapers cannot be found, the sad victims like many others of time and human carelessness. A lot of history has been lost with missing newspapers.

The author of the story and poem now is found to be Salathiel Curtis Coffinberry (1809-1889). The man, however, who discovered this newspaper in 1946, D.W. Garber, credited it to Salathiel's brother Andrew, born in 1788. Andrew Coffinberry made quite a name for himself throughout northern Ohio as a traveling lawyer, a flashy dresser, a raconteur, and later as a newspaper publisher. He went out of his way to stand out, especially in 1842 when he wrote an epic poem, "The Forest Rangers." The 200-plus pages in book form told a story of General Anthony Wayne on the Ohio frontier. It was popular primarily because of Andrew's reputation, and recently it has been reprinted. However, it was his only piece of published prose or poetry verified today.

The true Gottfried, the author of the earliest known John Chapman stories, was recently discovered from a rather obscure article that appeared in the *Ohio State Journal* (Columbus) in October 1839, which critiqued *The Hesperian*, one of many magazines of fact, fiction, and poetry published at that time.

While not crazy about the magazine or the poetry, the unidentified *Journal* author wrote that Gottfried was a friend, S.C. Coffinberry, who had published a sympathetic poem in the last issue, "The Song of Chin-gach-gook. The Last of the Mohicans." James Fenimore Cooper's book had first appeared in 1826.

Figure 7. Salathiel Coffinberry.

The *Journal* author went on to describe Salathiel as "one of the patriot heroes, and the bravest of them, who, last winter made the attack on the Canadian British at Windsor [The Patriot War]. He has exchanged the sword for the goose quill, and seems to be quite as much at home, in wooing the muse, as in cutting the throats of the Queen Victoria's red-coated soldiers." At that time he also happened to be practicing as a lawyer in Canal Dover, Ohio, having learned the trade from his oldest brother, Andrew.

According to much later writings of another elder brother, Salathiel was just a baby on his mother's lap in 1809, the second youngest of 10 children, when the Coffinberry wagon pulled into a very sparse Mansfield that had been officially laid out the year before. Their father, George, had been intrigued by the promise of a new town when they lived south in Lancaster, Ohio, and perhaps encouraged by the prospect of prosperity, his family arrived to find one abandoned log cabin. The building had served as a house, store, and tavern, once housing a man who set up shop for new settlers but was thrown out for drinking and questionable dealings with Indians. This lone cabin was much too small for the Coffinberry family, then consisting of 14 people, including in-laws and babies.

Figure 8. The Coffinberry Cabin in 1808 was considered one of the first houses in Mansfield.—Courtesy Mansfield Bicentennial Committee.

One of the sons-in-law was a printer, John Creyton Gilkison, who later published the *Richland Jeffersonian*, where the stories of Salathiel Coffinberry (then all grown up) appeared. He briefly published the first newspaper in Mansfield, the *Olive*, beginning in 1820, and before that the *Ohio Register* (1813-20) in the now defunct town of Clinton in neighboring Knox County.

Salathiel later wrote in an 1871 newspaper article, this time under his own name, about the first meal that night. Included with his family were town founders James Hedges and Jacob Newman, Jonathan Oldfield, Thomas Lofland, Michael Ruffner, James McClure, and John Chapman, later known as Johnny Appleseed. Salathiel was not old enough to remember the meal first-hand but probably heard about it second-hand. Coffinberry's 1871 article and the 1880 history by A.A. Graham are the only places the meal is mentioned.

It does seem fairly certain according to brother Wright, the family immediately threw up a temporary tent or "brush booth" on what became the southwest corner of the central square until their own larger log cabin was built. It doubled as an inn and tavern—feeding and serving the expected rush of pioneers into the wilderness.

The entire Coffinberry clan was described in the history books as extremely creative, genius even, a talent mostly credited to their mother, Elizabeth Little (Kline in German) Coffinberry. She told tales of links to royalty in Europe, and in 1833 she wrote a poem about the 1813 Levi Jones murder in Mansfield—she was there. Later it was said John Chapman ran for help but Mrs. Coffinberry did not mention him. He does, however, appear in memoirs of Wright and Salathiel, who claimed they had grown up with him.

Salathiel's rather lengthy Mansfield newspaper story in 1871 was a corrective response to the story in the national *Harper's Monthly* magazine that introduced Johnny Appleseed to the nation based on

Figure 9. Wright Coffinberry.

Richland County stories, but not necessarily stories according to the Coffinberrys.

Salathiel was described as "brilliant and eloquent" by his contemporaries, although often quixotic. His writing output, both prose, poetry and even music, far outweighed Andrew's. The titles of his prose were mentioned in the introductions to "The Massacre" and "The Battle" in the *Richland Jeffersonian*. The "Scenes at Medfield," is thought to be about Mansfield. Garber thought "Una-te-was-ka," was about the killing of the Wyandot Indian chief Toby in Mansfield in 1812.

Salathiel worked for a while as a lawyer in (Canal) Dover, Ohio, and it is possible these earlier stories appeared in Dover's Whig newspaper, the *Telegraph*, in the 1830s. Unfortunately, this newspaper is one of many that was published and since has just disappeared. Only one incomplete edition is known to exist today but includes nothing by Gottfried.

Newspaper stories sometimes were reprinted in other newspapers of similar viewpoint and some were just stolen. Only one of Gottfried's Medfield stories was found in Perrysburg's *Ohio Whig*, where Andrew and his son, James, lived in 1839. Using pseudonyms for the characters, it told about a sermon by a famed Methodist minister, the Reverend Russell Bigelow. Johnny Appleseed did not make an appearance here. Other surviving Ohio newspapers during this period have been searched, but nothing found.

After a brief war in Canada, Salathiel was back in Mansfield by 1841, probably earlier. Although there are no official records surviving of early Mansfield mayors, an 1879 article in the *Richland Shield and Banner*, says that Salathiel was a one-year-term mayor in 1841 before he and his family left in 1843 to follow another older brother, Jacob Wolf Coffinberry, to Constantine, Michigan. Wright moved to Centreville, Michigan, in 1844 and Grand Rapids in 1848. He, like Andrew, became an author much later in life. He left a detailed history of Mansfield in his journal, especially during the War of 1812. He did not include Chapman in wartime exploits but gave him a few general paragraphs of his own.

Salathiel, besides being a lawyer, was a bigwig in the Masonic lodge in Michigan. "The Swedenberger," however, was left behind in Ohio and never showed up again in his writings, as far as is known, until 1871. He said he remembered John Chapman well, because he was there—although 32 years had passed; but the author of the *Harper's* story, built on already written stories was not. Coffinberry was more accurate, he said.

But in 1839 he told a story based on what he himself had heard from friends and relatives. Remember, in 1812 Salathiel was only 3 years old. When he was 30, he called John Chapman "the Swedenberger," emphasizing religion over apples, and made him the first character to appear in "The Massacre" in the *Richland Jeffersonian*.

Presented in Chapter Five is half of the story. Someday we may find the rest. It is followed in Chapter Six by the second Swedenberger story, "The Battle," telling the tale of the 1812 Copus attack, and it is complete. Then in Chapter Seven is the 1871 report on Johnny Appleseed sent to the *Richland Shield and Banner* by Salathiel. It is true as far as Salathiel remembers it, and it does include some details not found anywhere else.

Chapter Four

The War of 1812

The War of 1812, as played out in Ohio, left an indelible mark on the Richland County pioneers, some of whom were still living in and around Mansfield in 1839 when Salathiel Coffinberry's articles began appearing in the *Richland Jeffersonian*.

It was a terrifying time, an uncertain time, but in retrospect it also could be an exciting time. Nobody had forgotten the fatal Indian attacks on the isolated cabins, but remembering them in print, in detail down to the conversations, sold newspapers. Maybe their memories were affected by what they read. At least the stories were likely to start some interesting conversations.

The Ohio frontier was a significant theater of this war with the English and its Indian allies on one side and pioneers and state militias on the other. Richland County was just north of the Treaty of Greenville line. White settlers to the south of this line were subject to recruitment into the military during the war. Richland County was part of the Indian territory, and its meager residents convinced the state they should stay at home to protect themselves from Indian attacks.

That did not stop the settlers from asking for help and for soldiers from the government when they needed them. The militia often occupied Mansfield as a result, but this also left Richland Countians vulnerable.

The early settlers were very nervous wherever they lived. The declaration of war was issued on June 18, 1812, but the war on the Ohio frontier began with the surrender of Fort Detroit by General William Hull on August 16, 1812. "Here come the British and Indians, from the north," the settlers thought.

The mostly agricultural and peaceful Delaware village of Greentown in Green Township, good neighbors up to this time, suddenly became a haven for hostile Indians, real or perceived. The Ohio militia decided the Delaware and some of their possessions should be moved to reduce the threat. This idea was not popular among the Indians; and the Reverend James Copus, who had preached to them at times and was considered reliable, was asked to convince the Indians they would be safer with other evacuees in Piqua.

On September 2, 1812, the Delaware were taken to the first stop on their journey, Mansfield. As the story goes, they had not gone far when they looked back and saw the soldiers burning their village. Maybe they blamed hostile militia who did not know them, but their faith in Copus and his cohorts vanished. Stories later were recounted that some of the Greentown Indians peeled off to join British allies.

In the many official accounts of the evacuation and burning nowhere is a John Chapman mentioned helping or defending the Indians. Moravian missionaries at that time talked about Greentown, both before and after, but never mentioned a John Chapman or Johnny Appleseed. Maybe he was invisible.

The militia and some of the settlers were still leery of any Indian and set up patrols at the drop of a rumor. A Wyandot chief, Toby, and his daughter reportedly had been staying at Greentown and were waylaid near Mansfield, and the father was savagely killed by white men. The daughter allegedly escaped to Upper Sandusky. The surviving descriptions were graphic and lingered in another newspaper story by Gottfried, "Una-Tee-Was-Ka," listed at the beginning of his Mansfield articles but never found. This name was included in "The Massacre" in a conversation between John Chapman and Kanochet. Garber concludes that Una-Tee-Was-Ka and Toby were the same. Another lost, bloody story. John Chapman may have been included in Gottfried's version, but never mentioned in any other.

The Gottfried stories we do have are of the Zeimer and Copus attacks. People at that time tended to huddle together for safety and were critical of settlers who chose to stay in their isolated cabin, such as those occupied by the Frederick Zeimer and James Copus families about 8 miles east of Mansfield. The Zeimer attacks and deaths by Indians came on September 10 and the Copus attack on September 15. These attacks were not fiction. They were reported in contemporaneous newspapers accounts and military reports. Surviving family members talked about them and the community remembered them. Accounts of the attacks eventually appeared in local history books and in newspaper history columns forever after. Monuments to those killed were raised and survive today on the location of the attacks. These attacks and deaths of both settlers and Indian were verified, but the details became jumbled.

Blockhouses were two-story log structures with the second story looming over the first, built by settlers and militia as protection against attacks. Mansfield had two that were built in the square shortly after the first two attacks. That is where the residents were hiding after Levi Jones, a shopkeeper, was killed by Indians on August 9, 1813, not so much a war casualty as an unfair-trade casualty.

The figure of Johnny Appleseed became wrapped up in these incidents, including at the beginning and end of the war, although there was little contemporaneous proof he was anywhere near. If he was in the neighborhood, it seemed compatible to his nature and religion that he would have helped. He is quoted in many history books as appearing at one crisis or another—Hull's defeat, the Zeimer and Seymour attacks, the Levi Jones killing, Perry's victory on Lake Erie—yelling in florid language as he ran through the woods.

The most likely story, and the one most accepted by modern historians, was that when Jones was killed the settlers took refuge in one of the blockhouses, and Chapman ran from Mansfield to Clinton, just north of Mount Vernon, to raise militiamen to return with guns. The *Ohio Register*, the only newspaper in the area and printed by John C. Gilkison, who had married a Coffinberry daughter, ran an account of a man alerting the community of the Mansfield attack, but did not say who:

> Tuesday evening, 10th Inst. An express arrived at this place from Mansfield, which place he had left at sunset – stated that the Indians had attacked that town killed and scalped a Mr. Jones – several men were missing. A number of mounted men from Clinton and vicinity have gone to their assistance.

This messenger, in later newspaper accounts and history books, became Johnny Appleseed.

The only account of the Levi Jones attack that came from someone who most likely was in Mansfield at the time is a poem from Elizabeth Little Coffinberry, Salathiel's mother, which appeared in a Mansfield newspaper in 1833 with no indication when it was written. It is quite long and detailed but does not mention Johnny Appleseed.

And it is interesting that Wright Coffinberry, in a journal written in his waning years, gives his brother, Andrew, the distinction of running to Clinton after Perry's victory. Running, or riding when there were paths, was the best way for settlers to urgently pass along bad or good news on the Ohio frontier.

They were often nameless.

Although the War of 1812 officially ended with the Treaty of Ghent in December 1815, the war ended for Ohioans, for all intents and purposes, on September 10, 1813, with the American victory in the Battle of Lake Erie. Wright Coffinberry, only six when it happened, said Mansfielders claimed to hear the cannon roar about 50 miles away on the northern coast in celebration.

So presented in the next chapter are Salathiel Coffinberry's versions, down to each colorful conversation, of the 1812 Zeimer and Copus attacks, appearing for the first time since they were printed in the 1839 and 1840 *Richland Jeffersonian*s. The hero was, conveniently, Johnny Swedenberger.

There is now no proof that he was in the cabins, or anywhere near Mansfield, when the attacks occurred, but it made for a good, and probably familiar, story. Although an embroidery that sold newspapers, the stories may contain more than just bits of truth, especially in the relationships among the characters.

Chapter Five

The Massacre

By the time the "The Massacre" was printed in 1839, John Chapman may have been generally known as Johnny Appleseed, but "the Swedenberger" (sometimes spelled Sweedenberger) was more or less a pseudonym, used exclusively by Salathiel Coffinberry. Similarly, Johnny was given another name by the Indians, Quan-quan or Prophet, apparently made up out of whole cloth by Salathiel as were other Indian names in these stories.

The Coffinberrys made a stab at Indian words, hearing such names when growing up in Mansfield, but apparently they were not very good at it. Later writings show a distinct sympathy, but the Indian names used in this and "The Battle," besides Kanotche, have never been found anywhere else, as in treaties or Moravian records.

But Salathiel also used thinly veiled pseudonyms for all his characters in "The Massacre." Readers of the *Richland Jeffersonian* had to have known who they were. Perhaps it was a courtesy, because many in this story of 1812 were still alive in 1839, including John Chapman. He died in 1845 in Indiana but is said to have visited Ohio after he had moved out. He may have read these and pondered why he found himself the hero of adventure stories.

Martin Ruffner appears in "The Massacre" as Michael Ruffner, actually the name of his brother; Rolin Weldon, Mansfield's first blacksmith, is Roley Wetmore; and a son, named here John, was really James. His friend, George Eldenberg,

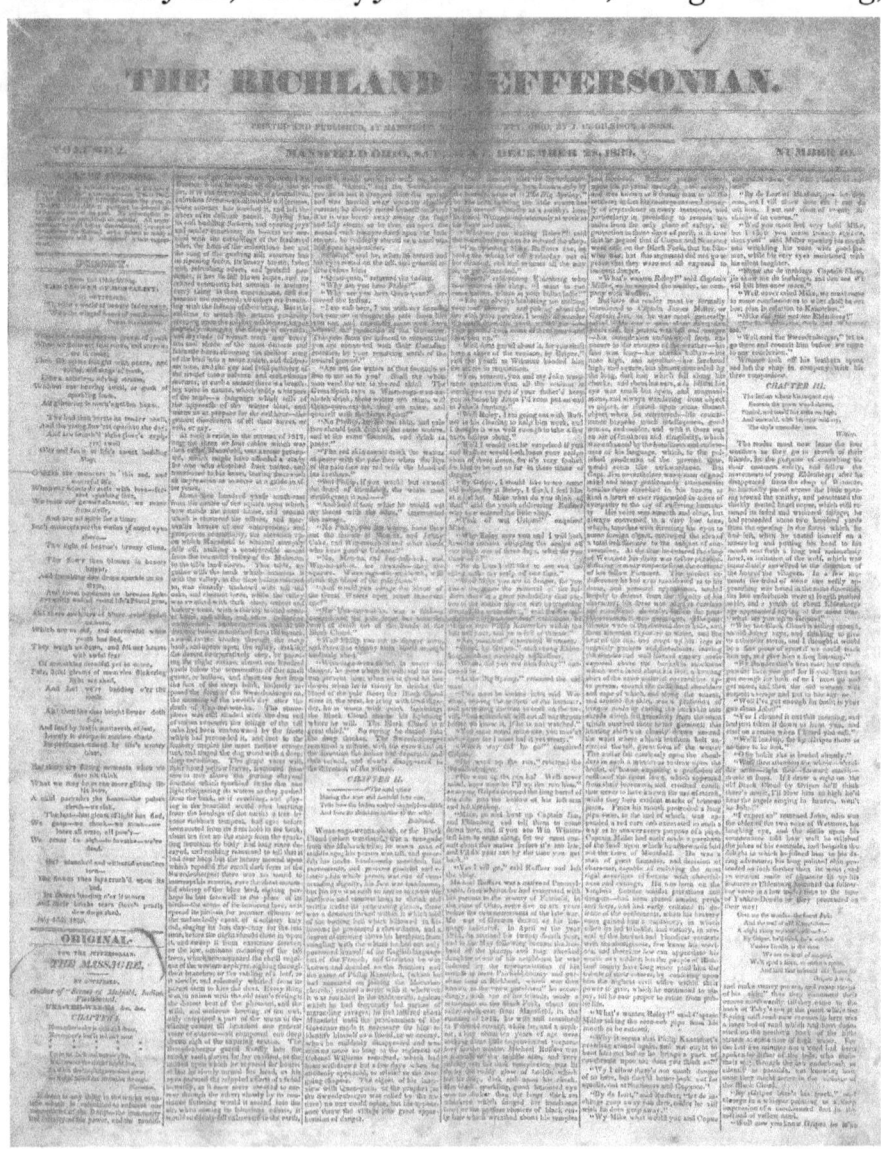

Figure 10. The *Richland Jeffersonian* dated December 28, 1839 with "The Massacre" (Garber's Copy).

was really Jacob Wolf Coffinberry, Salathiel's older brother who was 15 in 1812, from whom the author may have heard about the Indian-hunting hike in the woods.

Win Winters in the story is really the dapper Win Winship, and Captain Jim Miller is really James Hedges, one of three official surveyors of Richland County, considered a founder of Mansfield and a soldier of the War of 1812. His description is particularly detailed, and one can only hope accurate, because the appearance of historical figures does not get a lot of attention, especially without pictures. His only known likeness, according to a nephew, was destroyed in a fire in 1871, but Hedges lived until 1854 and was probably well known to Salathiel.

Unfortunately, John Chapman is not nearly as well described in this story as James Hedges. He is often called "old man," which is rather strange since Chapman, born in 1774, was only 37 in 1812. It may be Salathiel did not know how old he was, or he remembered him from his older years. Or Chapman may have looked old before his time, especially to a young boy. Running barefoot through the woods could do that to a person. His dress, so often reported in later stories, is not mentioned here, and he comes across as a calm, although indolent, educated, reasonable figure who fits in Mansfield nicely.

Strangely enough the Indian whom Johnny meets in "The Massacre" does not have a pseudonym. He consistently was known among historians and in history books as Philip Kanotche, his Moravian name. Although he is documented in historical records, he really could be any hostile Indian during this period of allegiance with England. He appears to be friendly enough to Johnny, who was thought to be highly regarded by Indians even that early.

John Chapman's allegiance in this tale, however, appears to be to the white settlers, because he quickly tells them of Kanotche's ominous presence. This Indian was a bad guy, because he appears later as such in various local histories. In this article he also draws attention away from the remnants of the more sympathetic Greentown Indians, Salathiel's friends, who had been evacuated from Richland County on September 2, 1812.

Kanotche appears in the opening scene of "The Massacre" as not an enemy of the Swedenberger but not a friend either. Johnny goes on to use this meeting in the woods as a warning to the Mansfielders clustered in the Weldon blacksmith shop.

Whatever remains in this article is a very revealing picture of pioneers, although there is no historical evidence anywhere that John Chapman was in Mansfield at this time or played any part in the subsequent Indian attack. However, he certainly makes an appealing addition to the cast of characters.

Unfortunately, the Coffinberry article, only half there, is primarily an adventure story set in the woods. The next weekly *Richland Jeffersonian* newspaper, which was expected to continue the story and the massacre, is now missing. Eventually the story would have included the events Richland Countians were well aware of and perhaps even remembered—the hostile Indian attack on the isolated Zeimer cabin and the deaths of settlers.

What Coffinberry had his Swedenberger do in the lost remainder of this story is now anybody's guess. Reprinted here is what remains of his newspaper account. Perhaps someday the rest will be found.

A complete original issue of the *Richland Jeffersonian*, Mansfield, Ohio, Vol. 2, No. 10, Saturday, December 28, 1839, can be found in the Western Reserve Historical Society Library in Cleveland, Ohio, possibly the donation of D.W. Garber of Mansfield, although the library has no such record.

All transcriptions in this book are verbatim as originally printed, including mistakes and archaic words and usages. Nothing has been changed.

The Massacre

By Gottfried
Author of "Scenes at Medfield," "Indian Punishment," "Un-Tee-Was-Ka," etc., etc.

CHAPTER I

November's sky is chill and dear,
November's leaf is red and sear.

Lo in its dark and narrow glen,
You scarce the rivulet might ken,
So thick the tangled greenwood grew,
So feeble trilled the streamlet through.
            Marmion.

If there is any thing in the works of nature which is calculated to enhance our conceptions of the Deity – the immensity and infinity of his power, and his munificence, and goodness which governed the Creator when he spoke all things into order, it is the contemplation of a boundless, unbroken forest – an illimitable wilderness when autumn has touched it, and left the traces of its delicate pencil. Spring has its soft budding flowers, and opening joys and tender emotions; its bowers are musical with the carrollings of the feathered tribe, the hum of the industrious bee and the song of the gushing rill; summer has its ripening fruits, its breezy breath, laden with refreshing odors, and grateful perfumes, it has its full blown hopes, and its refined emotions; but autumn is mature; every thing is then consummate, and the seasons are crowned; all things are breathing with the fulness of their being. But it is sublime to watch the autumn gradually creeping upon the mighty wilderness, imperceptibly changing the foliage of myriads and myriads of forrest trees into every tint and shade of the most delicate and fantastic hues; changing the mellow song of the bird into more sedate, and deliberate tone, and the gay and fitful pattering of the rivulet into a solemn and monotonous murmur; at such a season there is a breathing voice in nature, which softly whispers of the tomb – a language which tells of the approach of the winter blast, and warns us to prepare for the evil hour – the general dissolution of all thats sweet, or soft, or gay.

At such a crisis in the autumn of 1812, near the three or four cabins which was then called Mansfield, was a scene presented, which might have afforded a study for one who sketched from nature, and transferred to his heart, leaving there such an impression as to serve as a guide in after years.

About five hundred yards south-east from the centre of the square upon which now stands the court house, and around which is clustered the offices, and mercantile houses to our enterprising and prosperous community, the elevation upon which Mansfield is situated abruptly falls off, making a considerable ascent from the beautiful valley of the Mohican, to the table land above. This table, together with the bank which connects it with the valley, at the time before referred to, was densely timbered with tall old oaks and chestnut trees, while the valley was swathed with dark elms, walnut and hickory trees, with a thickly matted copse of hazel, and alder, and other indigeous under-brush. In the direction and at the distance before mentioned from the square, a small ravine breaks through the steep banks, and opens upon the valley, making the descent comparatively easy, by pursuing the slight ravine; almost one hundred yards below the termination of this small gutter, or hollow, and about ten feet from the foot of the steep bank, listlessly reposed the form of the Sweedenberger, on the morning of the twelfth day after the death of Una-tee-was-ka. The atmosphere was still shaded with the dun veil of Indian summer; the foliage of the tall oaks had been embrowned by the frosts which had preceeded it, and lent to the feathery maples the most mellow orange tint, and tinged the dog wood with a deep, deep vermillion. The grape vines with their broad yellow leaves, festooned from tree to tree above the purpling chrystal fountain which sparkled in the dim sun light checquering its waters as they gushed from the bank, as if revelling and playing in the beautiful world after busting from the bondage of the earth; a tree by some stubborn tempest, had ages before been rooted from its firm hold in the bank, about ten feet up the steep bank from the sparkling fountain; its body had long since decayed, and nothing remained to tell that it had ever been the mossy mound upon which reposed the small dark form of the Sweedenberger; there was no sound to interrupt his reveries, save the short mournful chirrup of the blue bird, sighing perhaps its last farewell to the place of its birth – the scene of its innocent love, as it spread its pinions for sunnier climes; or the melancholly croak of the solitary katy did, winging its last day-song for the last time, before the night should close in upon it, and sweep it from existence forever; or the low, ominous moaning of the tall trees, which accompanied the shrill requiem of the western zephyrs, sighing through their branches; or the rattling of a leaf, as it slowly, and solemnly whirled from its parent stem to kiss the dust. Every thing was in unison with the old man's feelings; the distant beat of the pheasant, and the wild, and ominous hooting of the owl, only composed a part of the moan of declining nature; all breathed one general voice of sadness – all composed one deep drawn sigh of the expiring season. The Sweedenberger gazed fixedly into the smoky vault above; he lay as silent, as the mound upon which he resposed for hours; at last he slowly turned his head, as his eye pursued the crippled efforts of a faded butterfly, as it once more assayed to career through the ether; slowly by its continued fluttering would it ascend into the air, when ceasing its laborious efforts, it would suddenly fall exhausted to the earth, again it would ascend into the ether; slowly but with no better result. "Amen," said the Sweedenberger as at last it dropped into the spring and was hurried away upon its rippling current; he slowly raised himself to watch it as it was borne away among the flags and lilly stems; as he thus sat upon the mound with his eyes fixed upon the little stream, he suddenly started as a hand was laid upon his shoulder.

"Philip!" said he, when he turned and his eyes rested on the tall, and graceful Indian before him;

"Quan-quan," returned the Indian.

"Why are you here, Philip?"

"Why are you here, Quan-quan?" returned the Indian.

"I am safe here, I am with my friends, but you are in danger; the pale faces like you not, and especially since you have refused the protection of the Governor. The pale faces are induced to suspect that you are connected with their Canadian enemies, by your removing north of the neutral ground."

"Are not the waters of that fountain as free to me as to you? Shall the white man vend the air to the red skin? The Great Spirit says to Wissa-saga-wen-na-eh-teh drink, these waters are mine, will Quan-quan say no, they are mine, and quarrell with the Great Spirit?"

"No, Philip, but the red skin, and the pale face should both drink from the same waters, and at the same fountain, and drink in peace."

"The red skin cannot drink the waters of peace with the pale face when the lips of the pale face are red with the blood of his brothers,"

"But Philip, if you would but extend the hand of friendship, the white man would grasp it and –"

Hold it fast; while he would cut my throat with the other," interrupted the savage.

"No Philip, you are wrong, have they cut the throats of Moo-na, and Johnny Cake, and Win-na-ash-ta, and other chiefs who have gone to Urbanna?"

"No, Moo-na, and John-neh-kek, and Win-na-ash-ta, are cowards – they are squaws. Wissa-saga-win-na-ah-teh will drink the blood of the pale faces."

"And would you avenge the blood of the Great Waters upon some innocent one?"

"No, Una-tee-was-ka was a fool – a coward, and the pale faces but took the work of death out of the hands of the Black Cloud."

"Well, Philip you are in danger here, and there has already been blood enough uselessly shed."

"Wissa-saga-win-na-ah-teh is never in danger, he goes where he will, and no one can prevent him; when he is tired he lies down; when he is thirsty he drinks the blood of the pale faces; the Black Cloud rises in the west, he is big with loud thunder, he is warm with quick lightning; the Black Cloud shoots his lightning where he will. The Black Cloud is a great chief." So saying he darted into the deep thicket. The Sweedenberger remained a minute, with his eyes fixed in the direction the Indian had departed, and then turned, and slowly disappeared in the direction of the village.

CHAPTER II

-----The aged crone
Mixing the true and doubtful into one.
Tells how the Indian scalped the helpless child,
And bore the shrieking mother to the wild.
                                   Brainard.

Wissa-saga-win-na-ah-teh was a renegade of the Mohawk tribe; he a man of middle age, his person was tall, and graceful; his limbs handsomely moulded; his movements, and gestures graceful and elastic; his whole person was one of commanding dignity, his face was handsome, but his eye was such an one to cause the hardiest, and stoutest heart to shrink and writhe under its penetrating glance, there was a deamon lurked within it which told of the boiling hell which billowed in his bosom; he possessed a shrewdness, and a degree of cunning above his brethren; from mingling with the whites he had not only possessed himself of the English language but of the French, and German; he was known and dreaded on the frontier; and the name of Philip Kanochet, (which he assumed on joining the Moravian church,) carried a terror with it wherever it was sounded in the settlements, against which he had frequently led parties of marauding savages; he had loitered about Mansfield until the proclamation of the Governor made it necessary for him to identify himself as a friend, or an enemy, when he suddenly disappeared and was seen no more so long as the regiment of Colonel Williams remained, which had been withdrawn but a few days when he suddenly appeared, as related in the foregoing chapter. The object of his interview with Quan-quan, or the prophet (as the Sweedenberger was called by the natives), no one could opine, but his appearance threw the village into great apprehension of danger.

Fifteen minutes after the Sweedenberger had left the spring, now known only by the homely name of "The Big Spring," he was seen entering the little square hut which served Witmore as a smithy; here he found Witmore industriously at work at his forge and anvil.

"What are you making Roley?" said the Sweedenberger as he entered the shop.

"I'm upsetting Mike Ruffner's axe, he broke the whole bit off yesterday out at his clearing and had to come all the way in, to get it mended."

"Roley," said young Eldenberg who now entered the shop, "I want to run some bullets, where is your bullet ladle?"

"You are always bothering me melting your lead, George, and poking about the fire with your powder. I would'nt wonder if a spark from the anvil would get into your powder horn some of these times and blow you up."

"Well don't growl about it, for you shall have a share of the venison, by Gripes," said the youth as Witmore handed the article in requisition.

"Yes, venison, you and my son John waste more ammunition than all the venison is worth you can get; if your father'd keep you at home by Jings I'd soon put an end to John's hunting."

"Well Roley, I am going out with Ruffner to his clearing to help him work, and I thought it was well enough to take a few extra bullets along."

"Well I would not be surprised if you and Ruffner would both loose your scalps some of these times, for it's very foolish for him to be out so far in these times of danger."

"By Gripes, I would like to see some old Indian try it, Roley, I think I feel him at it, ha! ha! Mike what do you thinks of that?" said the youth addressing Ruffner who now entered the little shop.

"Tink of wat Gripes?" enquired Mike.

"Why Roley says you and I will both have the Indians stripping the scalps off our heads one of these days, what do you think of it?"

"By de Lort I vill like to see von inching make my scalp off one time."

"Well Mike you are in danger, for you know that since the removal of the soldiers there is a great probability that parties of the hostile Indians will be trapseing through the settlement," said the Sweedenberger. "And besides," continued he, "I have seen Philip Kanotchet within the last half hour, and he is full of threats."

"Not possible!" ejaculated Witmore.

"Good, by Gripes," said young Eldenberg, winking cunningly at Ruffner.

"Where did you see him Johny?" continued he.

"At the Big Spring," returned the old man.

"This must be looked into," said Whitmore, ceasing the motion of the hammer, and permitting the iron to cool on the anvil, "that scoundrel will cut all our throats before we know it, if he is not watched."

"You must mend mine axe, you musn't shtop now for I must haf it yet areaty."

"Which way did he go?" enquired Gripes.

"He went up the run," returned the Sweedenberger.

"He went up the run ha! Well never mind, boys maybe I'll up the run him," so saying Gripes dropped the long barrel of his rifle into the hollow of his left arm and left the shop.

"Mike go and hunt up Captain Jim, and Eldenberg and tell them to come down here and if you see Win Winters tell him to come along, for we must consult about his matter before it's too late, and I'll fix your axe by the time you get back."

"Yes I vill go," said Ruffner and left the shop.

Michael Ruffner was a native of Pennsylvania, from whence he had emigrated with his parents to the county of Fairfield, in the state of Ohio, some five or six years before the commencement of the late war. He was of German descent as his language indicated. In April of the year 1812, he attained his twenty-fourth year, and in the May following became the husband of the plump, and rosy cheeked daughter of one of his neighbors; he was induced by the representations of his friends to leave Fairfield county and purchase land in Richland, which was then known as the "new purchase," he accordingly, with two of his friends, made a settlement on the Black Fork, about ten miles southeast from Mansfield, in the summer of 1812, his wife still remained in Fairfield county, while he, and a nephew, a boy about ten years of age were making some little improvement preparatory for the winter. Michael Ruffner was a man above the middle size, and very thickly set; his dark complexion was lit up by the ruddy glow of health, which left its deep, dark red upon his cheek. His black, sparkling, good humored eye was no darker than the large thickly set whiskers which fringed his handsome face; or the profuse clusters of black curly hair which wreathed about his temples and forehead. Ruffner prided himself upon his physical strength and activity, and was known as a daring man to all the settlers; in fact his courage savored strongly of imprudence in many instances, and particularly in persisting to remain ten miles from the only place of safety, or protection in those days of peril; it is true that he argued that if Copus and Seymour were safe on the Black Fork, that he likewise was; but this argument did not go to prove that they were not all exposed to imminent danger.

"What's wanten Roley?" said Captain Miller, as he entered the smithy, in company with Ruffner.

But here the reader must be formally introduced to Captain James Miller, or Captain Jim, as he was most generally called. He was a man about thirty-five years old. His person was tall and meagre – his complexion embrowned from exposure to the changes of the weather – his face was long – his cheeks hollow – his nose high, and aqualine – his forehead high, and square, but almost concealed by the long, dark hair which fell along his cheeks, and about his ears, *a la idian;* his eye was small but open, and magnanimous, and always wandering from object to object, or riveted upon some distant object when he conversed – his countenance bespoke much intelligence, good nature, and candor, and with it there was an air of frankness and simplicity, which was enhanced by the homliness and carelessness of his language, which, to the polished gentleman of the present time, would seem like awkwardness. But Capt. Jim nevertheless was a man of good mind and many gentlemanly attainments; besides there throbbed in his bosom as kind a heart as ever responded in tones of sympathy to the cry of suffering humanity. His voice was smooth and clear, but always conversed in a very low tone, which, together with directing his eyes to some foreign object, conveyed the idea of a total indifference to the subject of conversation. At the time he entered the shop of Wetmore his dress was rather peculiar, differing in many respects from the costume of his fellow Pioneers. The perfect indifference he had ever manifested as to his dress, and personal appearance, tended largely to detract from the dignity of his character; his dress was always careless and sometimes slovenly, but on the present occasion it was grotesque. His pantaloons were of the dressed deer hide, and from alternate exposure to water, and the heat of the sun, had crept up his legs and ungainly puckers and distortions, leaving the slender and well-formed ancle exposed above the buckskin mocksins which were laced about his feet; a hunting shirt of the same material covered his upper person, around the cuffs and shoulders and cape of which, and along the seams, and around the skirt, was a profusion of fringes made by cutting the buckskin into shreds which fell gracefully from the seam which attached them to the garment; this hunting shirt was closely drawn around the waist where a black leathern belt encircled the tall, gaunt form of the wearer. The collar fell carelessly upon the shoulders in such a manner as to draw open the breast, or bosom exposing a profusion of ruffles of the finest lawn, which appeared from their looseness, and crushed condition never have known the use of starch, while they bore evident marks of tobacco juice. From his mouth protruded a long pipe stem, to the end of which was appended a red corn cob excavated in such a way as to answer every purpose of a pipe. Captain Miller had early made a purchase of the land upon which he afterward laid out the town of Mansfield. He was man of great firmness, and decision of character, capable of enduring the most rigid severities of fortune with cheerfulness and courage. He was born on the Virginia frontier amidst privations and dangers – had been reared amidst perils and fears, and had early enlisted in defense of the settlements, when his bravery soon gained him captaincy, in which office he led to battle and victory, in several of the hardest and bloodiest contests of the aboriginese, few know his services, and therefore few can appreciate his worth as a soldier; but the people of Richland County have long since paid him the tribute of his esteem, by conferring upon him the highest civil office within their power to give, which he continued to enjoys, till he saw proper to retire from public life.

"What's wanten Roley?" said Captain Miller taking the corn-cob pipe from his mouth as he entered.

"Why it seems that Philip Kanotchet's prowling around again, and we ought to hunt him out before he brings a pack of cut-throats upon us; dont you think so?

"Wy I allow there's not much danger of us here, but they'd better look out for squalls, out at Seamore and Copuses."

"By de Lort," said Ruffner. "Let de inchings geep away von dere, odder he vill wish he does geep away."

"Wy Mike what would you and Copus and old Seymours do with a dozen of Indians?"

"By the Lort of Heafens, just let dem com, ant I vill show dem vot I can do mit him. I am not afrait of twenty inchings if he comes."

"Well, you must feel very bold Mike but I allow you twenty squaws, don't you?" said Miller opening his mouth and wrinkling his nose with good humor, while his very eyes moistened with his silent laughter.

"Show me de inchings Captain Shim, jis show me de inchings, and den see if I vill kill him once more."

"Well never mind Mike, we must come to some conclusions as to what shall be our best plan in relation to Kanotchet."

"Mike did you not see Eldenberg?"

"No I can him not find, and Winters too."

"Well said the Sweedenberger," let us go there and consult him before we come to any conclusion."

"Witmore took off his leathern apron and left the shop in company with his three companions."

CHAPTER III

> The Indian where his serpant eye
> Beneath the green wood shown,
> Started, and toss'd his arms on high,
> And answer'd, with his own wild cry,
> The sky's unearthly tone
> Wittier.

The reader must now leave the four worthies as they go in search of their friends, for the purpose of consulting for their common safety, and follow the movements of young Eldenberg; after he disappeared from the shop of Witmore, he hurriedly paced across the little opening around the smithy, and penetrated the thickly matted hazel copse, which still retained its faded and withered foliage; he had proceeded some two hundred yards from the opening of the forest which he had left, when he seated himself on a mossy log and putting his hand to his mouth, sent forth a long and melancholy howl, in imitation of the wolf, which was immediately answered in direction of the huts of the villagers. In a few moments, the tread of some one softly approaching was heard in the same direction, the low underbrush were at length pushed aside, and a youth of about Eldenbergs age approached saying at the same time, "What are you up to Gripes?"

"Why the Black Cloud is sailing around, so old Johny says, and thinking to give us a thunder storm, and I thought it would be a fine piece of sport if we would track him up, and give him a frog hoisting."

"By thunder that's first rate; how much powder have you got? For if you have not got enough for both of us I must go and get some, and then the old woman will suspect a scrape, and put in her say so."

"Well I've got enough for both; is your gun clean John?"

"Yes I cleaned it out this morning, and had just taken it down to hunt you, and start on a cruise when I heard you call."

"Well load up, for by Gripes there is no time to be lost."

"O by hokie she is loaded already."

"Well then attention the whole – shoulder arms – right face – forward march – music in front. If I draw a sight on the old Black Cloud by Gripes he'll think there's music, I'll blow him so high he'll hear the angels singing in heaven, won't he John?"

"I expect so" returned John, who was the elder of the two sons of Wetmore, his laughing eye, and the smile upon his countenance told how well he relished the jokes of his comrade, and bespoke the delight with which he joined him in his daring adventure, his long pointed chin protruded an inch further than its wont, and an unusual smile of pleasure lit up his features as Eldenberg hummed the following verse in a low under tone to the tune of Yankee Doodle as they proceeded on their way:

> Give me the woods – the forest dark,
>   And the trail of old Kanochet --
> A sight along my Old shellbark –
>   By Gripes, he'll think he's cotch it.
> Yankee Doodle is the tune
>   We are so fond of singing,
>   We'll spoil a horn, or make a spoon,
>   And kill that infernal Old Ingan By Gripes, Amen,

and make money purses, and razor straps of his skin; thus they continued their course northwardly till they came to the bank of Toby's run at the point where the Spring Mill road now crosses it; here was a large bed of sand which had been deposited on the southern bank of the little stream at some time of high water. For the last five minutes not a word had been spoken by either of the lads, who made their way through the low underbrush as silently as possible, not knowing how soon they might arrive in the vicinity of the Black Cloud.

"By Gripes here's his track," said George in a whisper pointing to a deep impression of a mockisoned foot in the soft bed of yellow sand.

"Well now you know Gripes he isn't far from here, for the track is right fresh yet."

"Well you see he's our meat, for we'll not quit his trail till we find him; let's move along slowly and keep a good look out; you see by the direction that he's made a bee line from the big spring, for the Sandusky trail, and our only chance is to overhall him before he gets far off, for as sure as the d---l He's got a pack of Indians within ten or fifteen miles of this, and you see he just come to see if the soldiers were gone before he would lead his hell-hounds upon us."

It were profitless for the reader to follow the two young men through their difficult course amidst the dense wilderness; the sun was seen like a large ball of fire through the smoky atmosphere at is was fast declining towards the western horizon. Wetmore and Eldenberg were still slowly, but cautiously making their way through the forest; suddenly Eldenberg, who proceeded Wetmore, as he was cautiously parting the brush in their way, dropped to the ground and in an instant his companion imitated his position.

"Did you see him Gripes?" enquired Wetmore as he slowly and silently drew to the side of Eldenberg.

"Yes by Gripes perch'd upon a high log, like a turkey on its roost."

"Where George? I'd like to see the old D---l too."

"Never mind – get your gun ready – see that your flint is in order, and your priming good; I'll let old Shellbark speak to him first, and if it misses then you many try him a blizzard."

"No Gripes, now I'll be dogged if that's fair – you know you won't miss him, so I'll have no share of the fun after all."

"Well, I'll tell you John," said Eldenburg, "we'll both shoot at once, and divide the honor between us; what do you say to that?"

"Well, I'm agreed, that's about fair."

"Well, now mind, I'll give the word one – two – three; – at the word of three pull away, now are you ready?"

"Yes."

"Well then raise up slowly, and draw your sight, for I shan't wait long."

The two young men raised slowly from the ground, and perceived about seventy-five yards before them the broad shoulders of Kanotchet, as he sat with his back towards them on a high log, which was bowed up in the centre some four or five feet above the underbrush below it.

"One – two – three, --" said Eldenburg. Click went both fire-lock in the same instant but without discharging either piece; Kanotchet dropped from the log into the deep thicket simultaneously with the noise produced by the flints of the rifles.

"Gone by hokie," said Wetmore gnashing his teeth in disappointment.

"H---l's fire what luck," said George, bringing the breech of his piece to the ground, so forcibly as to bury it several inches in the soft mould. "Let us follow him up, and perhaps we can get a shot at him before he gets out of sight yet George."

"Follow h----ll, I don't know what the d-----ls got into the guns both to miss fire at the same time; but let's see what can be done for him, perhaps we can get another chance at him."

After putting new flints into either lock, they again commenced the pursuit after Black Cloud. They had not proceeded more than a mile further when they came to a low valley, or wet bottom which was traversed by a small muddy creek, almost concealed by the thick alder bushes which lined its bank, while the stout sicamores tossed their white arms above them, as if to guard them from the tyrant tempest, which so frequently swept this particularly region in early times; innumerable fresh tracks, and trails of the savages traversed at a large log laying across the little stream upon which they had crossed.

"Thunder and Mars," said Eldenberg halting at the creek, "what do you think of that John?"

"Think! why I think the wigwams are within a half a mile of this, and that we had better be getting home, for the purpose of putting the people upon their guard for there is a considerable force here, and the intention I have no doubt is to make an attack shortly."

"Yes but don't you think we had better creep into this old sicamore log till night and then steal upon them and give them one h---ll of a blizzard, and make for home as fast as we can? You know we can out run them, and get home in time to prepare to receive them if they should follow us; but I dont believe they would follow us, if we would fire on them and kill a couple of them, I believe they would think, there was a considerable body had followed them, and would make off as fast as they could."

"Well I guess" returned Wetmore that would be as good a plan as any. I want to have a pop at them any how, and I don't care much whether they run or not, or what they do afterwards so I get a fair chance at one of them."

"Well you see the sun's nearly down, and we wont have long for — hark — hark — by Gripes, there they are; slip into the hollow log."

The two young men had scarcely concealed themselves within the hollow of the sicamore by which they stood during their short colloquy, till the tall form of the Black Cloud appeared on the opposite side of the little stream; the muzzle of the two rifles of Wetmore and Eldenberg were at once presented through a small aperture in the hollow log which afforded them so secure a retreat.

"One" – whispered Eldenberg as they both sighted along their rifle barrels after bringing them to bear upon the broad chest of Kanotchet;

"Two" already their fingers were pressed upon the springs of their fire arms, which would in another moment have sent the whistling lead through the bosom of the dark warrior, and have sent his dark spirit into scenes unknown.

"By Gripes hold on," said the wary young Eldenburg as two more larger warriors joined Wiss-saga-wem-na-eh-teh as he stood upon the bank; he made a gesture to the log which lay across the little stream, as another, and another made their appearance behind them; thus warrior after warrior, emerged from the thicket, till thirty had appeared and crossed the creek, passing within four feet of the spot where the two young pale faces lay concealed. The Black Cloud still remained on the spot where he was first discovered by the young men, and not more than forty feet from them; his countenance with over-shadowed with a deep gloom, a deep and horrid frown upon his brow gave his aspect the scowl of a demon; his eye seemed fixed upon vacancy, as he leaned his broad shoulder against the trunk of a large sicamore; thus he stood till the tramp of his comrades was indistinctly heard in the distance; already the two young adventurers had several time exchanged meaning glances which were thoroughly understood by either – once more their thumbs rested on the locks of their rifles, while a smile played over their features – again they glanced along their rifles, the breeches of which suddenly dropped from their cheeks, as their ears were saluted with the loud, shrill buzzing of a rattle snake. Kanotchet suddenly aroused from his reverie, he hurriedly glanced from side to side for an instant, till at last his features assumed a more hellish scowl, as his eye rested upon the fold of a large serpamt which lay coil'd within two feet of him, his eyes shot forth flash after flash of angry lightening as seized a stick, and slowly and cautiously approached the serpant – his weapon was uplifted, and with all his strength he brought it down towards the reptile, but the dry stick broke in his hands, and fell harmlessly at his feet, as the large mottle serpant darted upon him; with the agility of an antelope he sprang aside, clearing the low bushes for the distance of ten feet at one bound – but he as suddenly rushed forward again, as the angry buzz of another serpant assailed his ear from the very same spot upon which he stood; as he again leaped over the bushes, the glossy, golden length of a large snake was seen hanging to the lapell of his mockosin – his eye sparkled with supernatural horror, as he lit within two feet of the spot where his first enemy still reared himself in glistening folds, daring his red tongue like angry, forked lightning towards the Black Cloud, who stood a moment in fixed counsternation – his fingers grasped convulsively – the blood rushed to his forehead, till every vein was distended almost to bursting – his dark baselike eye emitted flashes, only equal in deadliness by the grim, carbuncke eyes of the serpant before him, which was preparing for another deadly onset, while its mate was twining in golden wreaths around his legs, and feet – a short shriek like that of one in the last agonies of death issued from the dark warrior as the reptile again darted forward, and clung to the bosom of his leathern hunting shirt – he seized it with both his hands, and dashed it from him, as he again sprang into the air, carrying with him the long, dangling form of the one which clung harmlessly to his foot – as he again struck the ground, with one effort he shook the mockosin, into which its fangs were fastened, from his foot, and with bound cleared the small creek – a prolonged shout of triumph succeeded, which was answered by his distant friends, and like a bounding deer, he was soon buried in the forest clearing the underbrush at every bound.

Fifteen minutes after the Black Cloud had disappeared, Witmore and Eldenberg withdrew from their retreat, and commenced the pursuit of their enemy, which, after proceeding a mile or two in the direction of Mansfield suddenly turned toward the north; at which point in their trail the two young men abandoned the pursuit, and silently sought their homes.

(To be continued next week)

[The newspaper issue with the continuation of this story has never been found.]

Chapter Six

The Battle

This is the second story by Gottfried, or Salathiel Coffinberry, that appeared in the Mansfield newspaper, the *Richland Jeffersonian*, on March 28 and April 4, 1840, and deals with the Indian attack on the James Copus cabin, about eight miles from Mansfield.

Some characters are only called by their first name, suggesting this may have been part of a series, but the intervening papers between the end of the first installment of "The Massacre" on January 4, 1838, and the beginning of "The Battle" are missing. The two young men who were so prominent in "The Massacre," George Eldenberg (Jacob Wolf Coffinberry) and John Witmore (James Weldon), and the acclaimed pioneer Captain Miller (James Hedges) continue to be called (once) by their pseudonyms in "The Battle" but the Copus family retained their real names. Ziemer was Seymour, one of several interpretations of the name. James Copus retained his real name, but his children, as many as nine, were not presented realistically. The eldest girls' names were changed, and the rest disappeared in this story. All really were at the attack and told about the screams for many years. But all survived, and their descendants still gather annually, usually in Ashland County, for the Copus Family Reunion.

The only other name in this story that changed was that of the soldier Isaac Die who was really George Dye. His interesting association in the article to the Swedenberger is unconfirmed. Eldenberg and Witmore are an attractive link between stories—maybe because they were young and mobile themselves. Johnny was middle-aged and mobile.

Copus was said by local historians to be highly regarded as a preacher to the Delaware Indians of Greentown and was called out by the militia on September 2, 1812, to convince them to abandon their village. He may have been blamed, although not directly, for the village being burned. Days after the burning, Copus was still in the neighborhood, but the militia were not, thus making him an easy target.

Coffinberry portrays Copus in his story in quite a negative light, and about 20 years older, which makes him an unsympathetic character in regard to the Indians but also to John Chapman (the Swedenberger) with whom he argues religion. The historical Johnny Appleseed was not argumentative. Here he does not get angry but stays determined in what he believes, an aspect often attributed to him.

In "The Battle," the Swedenberger is too likely to grab a rifle—or kill an Indian. He was a pacifist, who would not even harm a bug. Copus is described in detail, like Captain Miller in the first story, which may indicate Salathiel, who was only 3 years old at the time of the attack, got some details from older members of the community or his own family.

Johnny is described as dressed in tatters, an early description of his appearance, and his fleetness supports the public view that he was valued mostly as a courier, a messenger for the settlers. While John Chapman often is portrayed as very concerned about the well-being of his fellow man, here the Swedenberger is the hero, and thus more aggressive and willful than usually represented.

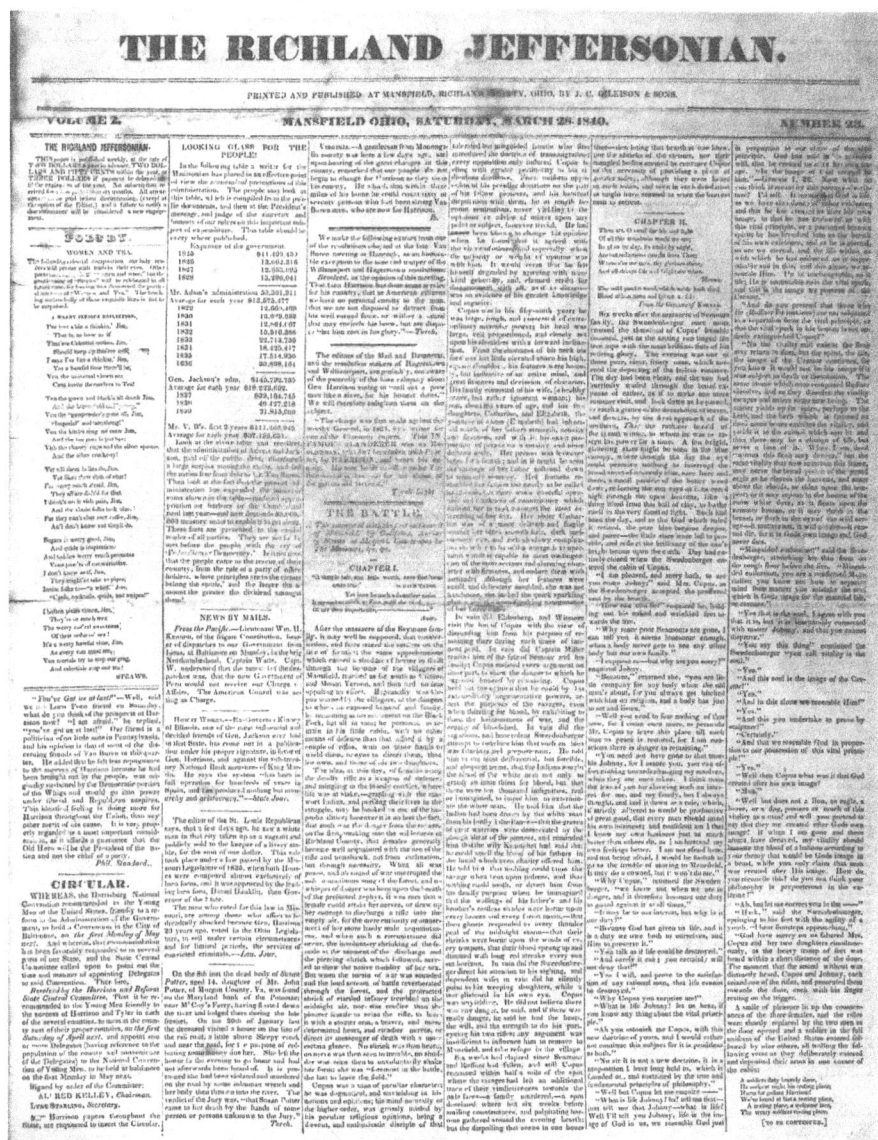

Figure 11. The *Richland Jeffersonian* dated March 28, 1840 with "The Battle."

All transcriptions in this book are verbatim as originally printed, including mistakes and archaic words and usages. Nothing has been changed.

The *Richland Jeffersonian*, Mansfield, Ohio, Vol. 2, No. 23, Saturday, March 28, 1840. Publisher: John Creyton Gilkison:

THE BATTLE

A tale connected with the first settlement of Mansfield

By Gottfried

Author of "Scenes of Medfield," "Una-te-was-ka," "The Massacre," etc., etc.

CHAPTER I

A simple tale, and little worth, save that
'twas owre true!
      Scotch Tales.

Yet bore he such a dauntless mein,
It seemed to mock at Fate, until she tired
Of her own importance ...."
      Anon.

After the massacre of the Seymore family, it may well be supposed, that consternation, and fears seized the settlers on the line of the frontier; the same apprehensions which caused a shudder of horror to thrill through the bosoms of the villagers of Mansfield, reached as far south as Clinton and Mount Vernon, and then had no less appaling an effect. Repeatedly was Copus warned by the villagers, of the dangers to which he exposed himself and family, by remaining at his settlement of the Black Fork, but all in vain; he persisted to remain in his little cabin, with no other means of defence than that afforded by a couple of rifles, with no other hands to wield them, or eyes to direct them, than his own, and those of his two daughters.

The idea, at this day, of females using the deadly rifle as a weapon of defence, and mingling in the bloody conflict, where life was at stake, -- grappling with the stalwort Indian, and periling their lives in the struggle, may be booked as one of improbabilities; however it is no less the fact. That such was the danger from the savages on the first breaking into the wilderness of Richland County, that females generally became well acquainted with the use of the rifle and tomahawk, not from inclination, but necessity. When all was peace, and no sound of war interrupted the soft monotinous song of the forest, and no whisper of danger was bore upon the breath of the perfumed zephyr, it was rare that a female could strain her nerves, or draw up her courage to discharge a rifle into the empty air, for the mere curiosity or amusement of her more hardy acquaintances, and when such a circumstance did occur, the involuntary shrinking of the female at the moment of discharge and the piercing shriek which followed, served to show the native timidity of her sex. But when the tocsin of war was sounded and the loud scream of battle reverberated through the forest, and the protracted shriek of startled infancy trembled on the midnight air, none was readier than the pioneer female to seize the rifle, to level it with a stouter arm, a braver, and more determined heart, and steadier nerves, or direct its messenger of death with a more certain glance. No shriek was then heard, no nerve was then seen to tremble, no shudder was seen then to unvoluntarily shake her form; she was "foremost in the battle, and the last to leave the field."

Copus was a man of peculiar character; he was dogmatical, and unyielding in his notions and opinions; his mind naturally of the highest order, was grossly misled by his peculiar religious opinions, being a devout, and enthusiastic disciple of that tolerated but misguided fanatic who first introduced the doctrine of transmigration; every opposition only induced Copus to cling with greater pertinacity to his ridiculous doctrines. From uniform opposition to his peculiar doctrines on the part of fellow pioneers, and his habitual disputation with them, he at length became sententious, never yielding to the opinions or advice of others upon any point or subject, however trivial. He had never been known to change his opinion when he found that it agreed with the views of others, and especially when the majority or weight of opinion was with him. It would seem that he felt himself degraded by agreeing with mankind generally, and, claimed credit for disagreement with all, as if to disagree was an evidence of greater knowledge and segacity.

Copus was in his fifty-ninth year; he was large, rough, and possessed of extraordinary muscular power; his head was large, well proportioned, and closely set upon his shoulders with a forward inclination. From the shortness of his neck his face was but little elevated above his high, square shoulders, his features were homely, but indicative of an active mind, and his great firmness and decission of character. His family consisted of his wife, (a healthy, active, but rather ignorant woman), his son, about ten years old, and his two daughters, Catharine and Elizabeth, the younger of whom (Elizabeth) had inherited much of her fathers strength, activity and firmness, and with it, his exact proportion of person on a smaller and more delicate scale. Her person was however large for a female; and in it might be seen the image of her father softened down to womanly symetry. Her features resembled her fathers too nearly to be called handsome, but there was a cheerful openness and frankness of countenance which entitled her to rank amongst the most interesting of her sex. Her sister Catharine was of a more delicate and fragile mould; her black smooth hair, dark meloncholy eye and rich shadowy complexion show her to be of that energetic temperament which is capable to meet contingencies of the most serious and alarming character with firmness, and endure them with fortitude; although her features were small, and delicately moulded, she was not handsome, she lacked the quick sparkling glance and the open speaking countenance of her fairer sister.

In vain did Eldenberg, and Witmore visit the hut of Copus with the view of dissuading him from his purpose of remaining there during such times of iminent peril. In vain did Captain Miller remind him of the fate of Semour and his family; Copus resisted every argument on their part, to show the danger to which he exposed himself by remaining. Copus held out the opinion that he could by his extraordinary argumentative powers, arrest the purposes of the savages, even when thirsting for blood, by exhibiting to them the heineousness of war, and the cruelty of bloodshed. In vain did the sagacious, and benevolent Sweedenberger attempt to convince him that such an idea was falacious and preposterous. He told him in the most defferential, but forcible, and eloquent terms, that the Indians sought the blood of the white man not only to gratify an inate thirst for blood, but that there were ten thousand indignities, real or imagined, to impel him to exterminate the white man. He told him that the Indian had been driven by the white man from his lordly inheritance – that the graves of their warriors were dessicrated by the plough shear of the pioneer, and reminded him that the wily Kanotchet had said that he could smell the blood of his fathers in the bread which even charity offered him. He told him that nothing could tame the savage when bent upon redress, and that nothing could sooth, or divert him from his deadly purpose when he imagined that the wailings of his father's and his brother's restless shades were borne upon every breeze and every forest moan, — that their ghosts responded to every thunder peal of the midnight storm — that their shrieks were borne upon the winds of every tempest, that their blood sprung up and dimmed with long red streaks every sun set horizon. In vain did the Sweedenberger direct his attention to his sighing, and dependent wife; in vain did he silently point to his weeping daughters, while a tear glistened in his own eye. Copus was unyielding. He did not believe there was any danger, he said, and if there was really danger, he said he had the heart, and the will, and the strength to do his part, eyeing his two rifles; any argument was insufficient to influence him to remove to Mansfield, and take refuge in the village.

Six weeks had elapsed since Seamour and Ruffner had fallen, and still Copus remained within a half a mile of the spot where the savages had left an additional trace of their vindictiveness towards the pale faces—a family murdered, —a spot desolated where but six weeks before smiling countenances, and palpitating bosoms gathered around the evening hearth; but the despoiling that scene in one hours time – desecrating that hearth at one blow, nor the shrieks of the victims, nor their mangled bodies seemed to convince Copus of the necessity of providing a place of greater safety, although they were heard in such tones, and seen in such desolation as might have seemed to warn the bravest man to retreat.

CHAPTER II

Thou art, O God! the life and light
Of this wondrous world we see;
Its glow by day, its smile by night,
Are but reflections caught of Thee;
Where e'er we turn, thy glorious shine,
And all things fair and bright are thine.
                              Moore.

The wild patriot band, which nobly hath shed
Blood of hangman and tyrant; so fell.
                    From the German of Korner.

Six weeks after the massacre of the Semours family, the Sweedenberger once more crossed the threshold of Copus' humble domocil, just as the setting sun tinged the tree tops with the most brilliant tints of his retiring glory. The evening was one of those pure, clear, frosty ones, which succeed the departing of the Indian summer. The day had been clear, and the sun had hurriedly waded through the broad expanse of eather, as if to make one more summer visit, and look down as he passed, to catch a glance of the devastation or leaves, and flowers, by the first approach of the northern, Thor the ruthless herald of the tyrant winter, to whom he was to resign his power for a time. A few bright, glittering stars might be seen in the blue canopy, where through the day the eye could perceive nothing to interrupt the broad sheet of heavenly blue, save here and there, a small particle of the butter weed down, reflecting the sun rays as it careened high through the open heavens, like a thing lifted from this ball of clay, to bathe itself in the very fount of light. Such had been the day, and as the God which ruled it retired, the pure blue became deeper, and purer – the little stars were left to preside, and reflect the brilliancy of the sun's bright beams upon the earth. Day had entirely closed when the Sweedenberger entered the cabin of Copus.

"I am pleased, and sorry both, to see you come Johny," said Mrs. Copus, as the Sweedenberger accepted the proferred seat by the hearth.

"How can that be?" enquired he, holding out his naked and wrinkled feet towards the fire.

"Why since poor Seamours are gone, I can tell you it seems lonesome enough, when a body never gets to see any other body but our own family."

"I suppose so – but why are you sorry?" enquired Johny.

"Because," returned she, "you are little company for any body when the old man's about, for you always get hitched with him on religion, and a body has just to set and listen."

"Well you need to fear nothing of that now, for I come once more, to persuade Mr. Copus to leave this place till such time as peace in restored, for I am conscious there is danger in remaining."

"You need not have gone to that trouble Johnny, for I assure you, you can effect nothing towards changing my resolves, when they are once taken. I think none the less of you for showing such an interest for me, and my family, but I always thought, and laid it down as rule, which, if strictly adhered to would be productive of great good, that every man should mind his own business; and confident am I that I know my own business just as much better than others do, as I understand my own feelings better. I am not afraid here, and not being afraid, I would be foolish to go to the trouble of moving to Mansfield. It may do a coward but it won't do me."

"Why, Copus," returned the Swedenberger, "we know not when we are in danger, and it therefore becomes our duty to guard against it at all times."

"It may be to our interest, but why is it our duty?"

"Because God has given us life, and it is a duty we owe both to ourselves, and Him to preserve it."

"You talk as if life could be destroyed."

"And surely it can; you certainly will not deny that?"

"Yes I will, and prove to the satisfaction of any rational man, that life cannot be destroyed."

"Why Copus you surprise me!"

"What is life Johnny? let us hear, if you know anything about the vital principle."

"Ah you astonish me Copus, with this new doctrine of yours, and I would rather not continue this subject for it profitless to both."

"No sir it is not a new doctrine, it is a proposition I have long held to, which is founded on, and sustained by the true and fundamental principles of philosophy."

"Well, but Copus let me enquire – "

"What is life Johnny? ha? tell me that – just tell me that Johnny – what is life? Well I'll tell you Johnny, life is the image of God in us, we resemble God just in proportion to our share of the vital principle. God has said in his revealed will, that he created us after his own image. 'In the image of God created he him.' Genesis 1, 22. Now what do you think is meant by this passage of scripture? I'll tell. It means that God is life, as we have abundance of other evidence; and that he had created us after his image, in that he endowed us with this vital principle, or a portion of his spirit; he has breathed into us the breath of his own existence, and as he is eternal, so are we eternal, and the life within us with which he has endowed us imperishable and in this, and this alone, we resemble Him. He is unchangeable, so is life; He is immutable so is the vital spark, and this is the image we possess of the Creator."

"And do you pretend that those who die (Ruffner for instance) are not subjected to a separation from the vital principle, or that the vital spark in his bosom is not entirely extinguished Copus?"

"No the vitality still exists; the flesh may return to dust, but the spirit, the life, the image of the Creator continues, for as you know, it would not be his image if it was subject to death or dissolution. The same atoms which composed Ruffner dissolve, and as they dissolve the vitality escapes and enters some new being. The matter yields up its spirit, perhaps to the herb, and the herb, which is fattened on dead mens bones embodies the vitality, and yields it to the animal which eats it; and thus there may be a change of life, but never a loss of it. When I am dead 'worms this flesh may devour,' but the same vitality that now animates this frame, may nerve the broad pinion of the brave eagle as he cleaves the heavens, and soars above the clouds, or rides upon the tempest; or it may repose in the bosom of the snow white dove, as it floats upon the summer breeze, or it may throb in the breast, or flash in the eye of the wild savage – it matters not, it will not die – it cannot die, for it is Gods own image and God never dies."

"Misguided enthusiast!" said the Swedenberger, stretching his thin form on the rough floor before the fire. "Misguided enthusiast, you are a confirmed Materialist; you know not how to separate mind from matter; you mistake the soul which is Gods image for the material life, or essence."

"Yes that is the soul, I agree with you that it is, but it is inseparably connected with matter Johnny, and that you cannot disprove."

"You say this thing," continued the Swedenberger "you call vitality is the soul."

"Yes."

"And this soul is the image of the Creator?"

"Yes."

"And this alone we resemble Him?"

"Yes."

"And this you undertake to prove by scripture!"

"Certainly."

"And that we resemble God in proportion of our possession of this vital principle?"

"Yes."

"Well then Copus what was it that God created after his own image?"

"Man."

"Well but does not a lion, an eagle, a horse, or a dog, possess as much of this vitality as a man? and will you pretend to say that they are created after Gods own image? If when I am gone and these atoms have decayed, my vitality should become the blood of a baboon according to theory that would be Gods image in a beast, while you only claim that man was created after His image. How do you reconcile this? do you not think your philosophy is preposterous in the extreme?"

"Ah, but let me correct you in the—"

"Hark," said the Sweedenberger, springing to his feet with the agility of a youth. "I hear footsteps approaching."

"God have mercy on us faltered Mrs. Copus and her two daughters simultaneously, as the heavy tramp of feet was heard within a short distance of the door. The moment that the sound without was distinctly heard, Copus and Johnny, each seized one of the rifles, and presented them toward the door, each with his finger resting on the trigger.

A smile of pleasure lit up the countenances of the three females, and the rifles were shortly replaced by the two men as the door opened and a soldier in full uniform of the United States entered followed by nine others, all trolling the following verse as they deliberately entered and deposited their arms in one corner of the cabin:

> A soldiers duty bravely done,
> He seeks at night his resting place;
> Hurra for Gallant Harrison!
> We've found at last a resting place,
> A resting place, a welcome face,
> The weary soldiers resting place.

(To be continued)

Richland Jeffersonian, Mansfield, Ohio, Vol. 2, No. 24. Saturday, April 4, 1840:

Chapter III

Prepare yourselves, therefore, and put yourselves into such an agreeable posture that you may be ready to fight with the enemy as soon as it is day to-morrow morning.

Josephus.

"This is as good as a feller cou'd expect, Isaac, don't you think so?" said one of the soldiers addressing one of his companions, after they had been seated around the comfortable fire crackling before them. The soldier addressed was a young man perhaps not more than twenty, and although the youngest of the company, seemed to be regarded by his companions with marks of respect. He was of the middle stature, well formed, and possessed the countenance, and eye of a soldier.

"Yes," said he after musing nearly a minute, "yes, this is a much better place of rest that we could have expected after a long, and tedious march through the swamps."

"Nothing is wanting now to make you comfortable, soldiers, but a good warm supper, which our women shall soon prepare for you," said Copus, cordially, as he added another stick to the fire.

"No sir," said the young soldier, "it is enough for us to meet with so cordial a reception as you have afforded us; we have our rations in our knapsacks, and we think it a sufficient favor to be permitted to lay before your fire for the night."

"Such fare," returned Copus, "as our homely cabin will afford is at your service, and I insist upon your acceptance of it."

"We appreciate you kind offer, but it could not be expected that so many hungry soldiers should be quartered upon you for the night, and invited to your board, likewise; or, is so, that they would leave much behind them to repay the kindness of their host."

"You must eat, you all must eat," returned Copus, "for it is our duty to do something for our country; I am too old to bear arms, myself, and it is as little as I can do to feed the hungry soldier, who has been defending the rights of his country, and to whom, perhaps I am partially indebted for the privilege I enjoy of offering it."

"Well sir, if you insist upon it, we will thankfully accept of your offer, but go to no trouble for us."

"I can assure you that our best effort will promise nothing extraordinary, for in this new country delicacies, and luxuries are out of the question; but let me enquire from whence you come, and where are you now going?"

"We are of the Pennsylvanians who volunteered to serve our county under Hull; his shameful surrender tells the balance of our story; we are on our way to our homes."

"What county are you from?" enquired the Swedenberger, still leaning against the wall, in the same posture which he first assumed upon the entrance of the soldiers, by whom he was till then unobserved, and then but indistinctly seen, owing to the dark shaddows of the solders thrown upon the spot he occupied."

"I am from Westmoreland county," said the speaker, "my comrades are from different counties in the western part of Pennsylvania."

"I am somewhat acquainted in Westmoreland county," returned the Swedenberger "may I enquire your name?"

"Isaac Die is my name," said the young man, directing his eye to the place where the Swedenberger still leaned against the wall, with his arm folded upon his bosom.

"I thought I knew your voice," said the old man coming forward.

"Is it possible this is you Johnny!" said Die, meeting the old man, and seizing his hand, which he shook long and hartily.

"Well, I am delighted to see you once more. It is a good while since you was in our way."

"I was at your fathers about a year ago, but you was not at home."

"Well, can't you go along with us now? We will divide rations with you, and if you put up with soldiers fare we will make you as comfortable as soldier's fare can make you."

"Ah! Isaac. I think you would find that I could put up with any kind of fare, if occasion required, and if I were to go I would not make your rations a morsal less. For I think it must be shiftless creature that cannot live on natures bounties, where they are so profusely scattered as they are in these forests; I have subsisted and can again subsist sumptuously in the woods, without any other fare tham that afforded by the hand of nature."

"Well, will you go?"

"I could be of no use to you to go Isaac, and here I may be of use, I would not mind to go to the Tuscarawas with you, for I want to get some apple-seeds at Goshen; and I want to see old Heckenwelder about my nursery there; he promised to take care of my trees, and I am told that the Goshen Indians have let their horses break in, and destroy them."

"Well you may as well go."

"I will determine by morning."

"Very well." So saying, Die now accepted the seat at the table, to which Copus had already invited him several times.

After due honor was paid by the soldiers, to Dame Copus' culinary skill, they one by one, spread their blankets upon the floor, and sought repose with the exception of Die, who for many hours after the family had retired, still occupied a rude stool before the fire, in low and earnest conversation with the Swedenberger, the broken, and detached portions of which caught by Copus, were insufficient to determine its purport, till long after the shrill clarion of Chanticleer had announced the midnight hour, and after the fire had been reduced, which now sent but an occasional dim flickering light through the rude apartment, when Die arose, and was heard to say as he erected his well knit form before the fire place "with such a chance I would very soon consent."

"No Isaac," returned the old man "I am willing to serve my country in any way that I can make myself useful, but I am not well enough skilled in the art of dissimulation to make a successful spy, even if I could get the consent of my own conscience to act deceitfully."

"Well, we will talk of it in the morning," said Die, wrapping his blanket around him, and taking a place on the floor, beside his sleeping companions.

"Johnny," said Copus, "throw another stick of wood upon the fire before you lay down, or the soldiers will be cold before morning."

The Swedenberger did as required, and then stretched his guant little form before the fire place, with no other covering to protect him from the frosty air which was already circulating through the cabin that the tattered garments which covered his person.

For some time after the Swedenberger lay down, all was as silent and still as if every living thing had sighed its last, save the heavy breathing of the soldiers, or the shrill monotinous whisper of the house cricket in the chimney; at length after the long, shrill cry like that of the boding owl had disturbed the stillness of the scene without, the Swedenberger arose, and sat thoughtfully before the fire until the hooting without was answered by a similar sound in another direction.

"There, Copus, do you hear that?" said the Swedenberger.

"Yes I do," answered Copus, turning in his bed.

"What does it mean, do you suppose?" continued the Swedenberger in a low voice.

"Nothing; the owls are screaming around that way every night."

"That was not the scream of an owl, in my opinion."

"Why Johnny, I suppose that you had heard owls hooting often enough to tell their voice when you hear it."

"I may be mistaken, Copus, but I thought that I had heard the whoop of the Indian often enough to tell it from the hooting of the owl."

"What!" said Copus, "scared at an owl, old man, come lay down. I thought you was a better soldier?"

"Copus I am not the man to shrink, or feel a shudder of fear, were I confident that it was the war whoop, from a thousand savage throats; but I may be mistaken, for heard the first of these cries but indistinctly, as I was asleep, however the last sound was much like an Indians imitation of cry of an owl."

"Well it was only an owl."

"Very well, then I'll lay down again," so saying the Swedenberger once more sought repose.

CHAPTER IV

"At once there rose as wild a yell,
Within that dark, and narrow dell,
As if the fiends from heaven that fell
Had peal'd the banner cry of hell."
~ Lady of the Lake.

The sun had risen, when Die, with three of his companions stooped over a spring within a few rods of the cabin of Copus, in the performance of their morning ablutions, when the unexpected "whugh" of an Indian from the bank above the springs, induced Die to raise himself from his stooping attitude, and turn his eyes in the direction of the sound, just as a rifle ball whistled past his ear, and brought down one of his companions struggling in the agonies of death, into the spring; the pure crystal waters of which were soon mingled, and discolored with the blood which gushed from the soldier's heart.

As Die arose he discovered at one glance the situation they were in; above the spring, on the little elevation from where the shot had been discharged, stood a low, thick-set, swarthy savage, reloading, while the smoke of his recently discharged piece wreathed in smoky coils around him, half concealing his hideously streaked, and painted features, which were rendered still more revolting by a glow of pleasure, as he quickly glanced alternately upon his rifle and the body of the soldier floundering in the spring. Behind him he discovered two other warriors with their tomahawk raised, and rushing upon them, with all that energy, and firmness which characterizes men when certain of success. "To the cabin! to the cabin!!" shouted Die as he saw his two remaining friends retreating towards an adjacent thicket, persued by the two Indians, while he hurried up the path which led to the cabin door. He kept his eye upon the savage above the spring till he heard another shout before him in the path, when to his surprised his eyes rested upon the stately form of a young warrior, far superior to him in size. Already the young warrior had his weapon poised, and was in the act of hurling it at the head of Die, who just discovered his enemy in time to stoop, and let the weapon pass over him. In a moment the young soldier had the tomahawk in his hand, and confronted his enemy, who lost not a moment in drawing his scalping knife, when he rushed upon the young man. As Die closed with the young warrior, he made an unsuccessful effort to wrest the knife from his hand, which however turned the blow from his bosom where it was directed; in doing this he lost his grasp of the tomahawk, and there stood defenseless before an enemy who he feared was his superior in point of physical strength; but there was no alternative left, he had to either grapple with the young warrior hand to hand, or at once fall his victim, the former of which he no sooner determined upon than he sprang like a tiger upon his enemy; the struggle was long and doubtful; Die felt that his efforts were unequal to the yet unimpaired strength of his antagonist, who was conscious of his superior powers; just as he was uniting his strength for one last effort, a shot from the Indian above the spring, intended for him, passed through his clothes, and lodged in the beast of his adversary who fell lifeless before him.

As the warrior fell a howl arose from the forest in every direction, which was echoed upon the morning air like the howlings of the damned; every tree and shrub, seemed to conceal a savage. The long mournful cry had ceased, and all was as still as if the voices of blood had never been sounded, when Die sprang forward to gain the cabin door; just as he turned around the corner of the cabin, and came in front of the building, another warrior met him; as quick as thought he buried the knife which he seized from his fallen enemy, before he rushed for the house, in the bosom of his new antagonist – he gained the door, but it was closed, and barred against him – he hammered at the door and shouted as he saw the forest darken by the swarthy forms of countless warriors, and as his ears was stunned by the deafning peal, or angry shout which arose from them, Several warrior sprang forward, and ran towards him, as a shower of bullets rattled harmless around him. The foremost savage was in a rod of the door, when just as he fell from a shot within, the door opened and Die entered the cabin, closing the door after him which was again immediately fastened.

When Die entered the cabin he found his comrades, with their pieces ready for immediate action, stationed at proper points within the small building for its defense; small apertures had been hastily made through the chinking upon the first intimation of danger which answered the purpose of port-holes. Copus was passing to and fro, and harranguing the soldiers, or upbraiding the Swedenberger who stood by the wall with his arms folded on his breast, apparently unconscious of what was passing with, while his eyes were directed through a crevice towards the forest, where the enemy was concealed. The daughters stood with rifles in their hands and cautiously glancing towards the woods. "No Johnny, you would be foolish to go now; you would never reach Mansfield alive, and I insist upon your remaining," continued Copus.

"I think Copus," said the Swedenberger, "That I could get to Mansfield and bring assistance before the Indians could do any great mischief with as good a defense as you have here, and it is certain that without some reinforcement we will all be sacrificed, as soon as it is dark enough for the Indians to steal up to the cabin unnoticed; they number more than a hundred, and they are headed by Kanotchet."

"That cannot be, for it well known that he died of wounds received in his fight with Ruffner; nor at least a friendly Indian told me so but a day or so since."

"Well, yonder he is now, you can see for yourself" said the Swedenberger, pointing to a group of Indians, who hurriedly passed from behind one thicket to another still nearer the house.

"Now Copus you are satisfied, and you know the enemy you have to contend with; once more I entreat you to let me out, and I will run the risk of getting to Mansfield and obtaining timely assistance. I know that it is a dangerous undertaking, but my life may as well be lost in such an effort, as to quietly remain here to be sacrificed."

"No Johney, I won't consent," returned Copus.

"Copus you are too self-willed; you speak for others who are as deeply interested as yourself, without consulting their feelings. If a majority of those in jeopardy agree with you; I will stay, and do what I can till the last drop of blood has sped; if not I will go. What say you all, time passes, shall I go?"

"O for Heaven's sake Johney do go, said the three women simultaneously, while the soldiers one and all negatived the good old man's proposition, from a conviction that he would never get a hundred yards from the house.

"That must be Kanotchet," said Die, glancing along his rifle at the head of Wissa-saga-wenna-eh-teh, as he cautiously raised his tall form above the low hazel brush of a thicket, within thirty yards of the cabin. Another moment his piece was discharged, and the giant form of the wily warrior sunk behind the bushes. A shout rent the cabin from its inmates, which was answered by a protracted howl from the savages without.

Every eye was bent upon the forest, which was yet reverberating the savage yell of the Indians, when several dark warriors were seen running across the little opening of several acres around the house, shouting "Quan-quan! Quan-quan! ho! ho!" at the top of their voices; every eye was turned in the direction of the point towards which the warriors were running, where was discovered the Swedenberger, bare headed, with his long black hair, and tattered garments streaming in the wind as he flew before his pursuers with the fleetness of youth.

"What a fool!" said Copus, turning and looking in vain through the apartment for the Swedenberger, I could not believe the evidence of my own eyes, was it not corroborated by the fact of the old fools absence."

"There they have got him at last," said Katharine, clasping her hands, and turning from the small aperture through which she had been steadily watching the progress of the chase. "They got the poor old creature at last," said she, as a loud shout arose from the savages, who were the moment before in the act of surrounding the old man."

"Father, father," said Katharine, "I see an Indian on a tree top."

"Well Kate do your duty like a soldier."

"O shall I shoot him father? must I shoot him? must I shed blood?"

"Do your duty Kate, for here is one making for the house in the opposite direction – and another, every one stand to their post, do your duty Kate, for none can come to your assistance."

"I see him," said the girl, from whose lips and cheeks the blood had receeded, leaving them as pale and ashy as the hue of death; "I see him – he is drawing up his gun," said she, pressing the breach of her rifle to her pallid cheek – he is aiming at some one father," continued the timid maiden, as she directed her sight along the glittering rifle barrel, and laid her long fore-finger on the trigger; "O father he will soon shoot – he is still there" continued she, pressing the trigger of her firelock vigorously. "O God I am a murderer," shrieked the maiden, as the piece was discharged and fell from her hands, while the heavy body of the savage plunged headlong from the top of the tall elm near the house, "I have killed a fellow being – I have shed blood! blood! blood! which called for blood, blood!" As Katherine pronounced these last words, she sunk upon a rude chair which stood behind her, where she remained in a state of apparent insensibility for some minutes. During this time Copus' attention was directed to a warrior who was rushing towards the door, he came with such speed as to entirely escape several shorts which were aimed at him from the soldiers within the little hut. He was already within two rods of the house when Copus hastily withdrew the bar, and threw open the door at the same time presenting and discharging his rifle at the daring savage, who upon its discharge uttered a short shriek , leaped convulsively into the air, and fell lifeless to the ground.

A long shout from Copus while he stood in the door reloading his piece, was succeeded by a groan, as he fell dead upon the threshold, from several balls which in the same moment entered, and lodge in his breast. Another shout of triumph around from the savages, which was interrupted by a volley of shots at the soldiers as they labored to draw the lifeless body of Copus into the house and close the door. Die suddenly sunk to the floor as he was in the act of closing the door, after having succeeded in drawing the corpse within.

"There's another dead man," said Mrs. Copus, as Die fell, and the shout of the savages in the wood once more swelled through the forest.

"Not dead yet," said Die, struggling to gains his feet. "Give me something, a shawl, or handkerchief to tie around my thigh, and I'll live yet to send some of you daring red skins to another world."

He hurriedly tied a handkerchief around his left thigh, which had received a ball, leaving a serious and painful wound. In this condition he resumed his post, where like a brave man, and true soldier, (no longer being able to stand,) he sat and did his duty.

"Kate, Kate to your gun, to your gun sister," shouted Elizabeth, why do you set there moping at such a moment?"

"I have blood enough, 'who so sheddeth man's blood by man shall his blood be shed,'" said Katherine, gazing vacantly into her sister's face.

"There is the blood of your lifeless father, does not that arouse you to revenge?"

"Our liveless father!" ejaculated the maiden, gazing wildly around her till her eyes rested upon the corpse of her father, when the blood rushed to her forehead and cheeks in a torrent, her eye flashed and her countenance lit up with supernatural wildness – she seized to rifle from beside her fathers body, and after wiping with her white apron the stains of blood from the glittering barrel, fervently kissed it exclaiming "that blood shall be avenged, so help me heaven." She flew to an apperture in the wall, in the front part of the small building.

The Indians emboldened by success now shew themselves (about fifty in number) about seventy five yards from the house, with the evident intention of making a desperate sally, and storming that place of refuge. The tall form of Kanotchet was seen running to and fro, making violent gestures, and haranguing his fellows.

"Now, now" said Die, "they are going to make a sally, and if they do we are gone; nothing but a well directed fire will prevent it; let every man bear upon them, and we can start them before they rush. Let me give the word and all fire as nearly together as possible, and load and fire as fast as possible as long as one of them remains.

Die's plan was pursued, and proved successful. The nine pieces were at one moment discharged into the crowd of Indians, several of them were seen to fall, and the balance, after discharging their pieces towards the house sought the woods in confusion.

A suppressed shriek issued from Elizabeth as she fell to the floor at the moment when the Indians discharged their rifles, before their retreat.

"Are you badly wounded sister?" said Katherine supporting her.

"My leg is shattered to atoms; help me to the bed, I am fainting," returned Elizabeth as the blood left her face, and she became insensible, in which condition she lay for many minutes.

The day was fast drawing to a close; the sun had already hid himself in the west, and the time was fast approaching when it might be expected that the enemy would take advantage of the darkness to make a successful attack upon the house. Every one stood at their post in deepest apprehension, till darkness had shut out every object from the vision.

"There they come," said Die in a loud whisper, "let us sell our lives dearly;" continued he as a rustling in the leaves was heard at a distance, like the noise of many feet. Slowly the sound approached until it was within a rod of the house which was as dark and silent as if not a breathing thing was there. "Shall we fire?" enquired one of the soldiers as the sound came within the range of the guns.

"No," returned Die, "save your shot till the last moment, for we cannot load again."

"Suddenly the tramp ceased, and all was still without as within. The hearts of the inmates of the cabin beat audibly in that dreadful moment of suspense.

"Too late – too late -- O what a pity," said a voice without.

"O! Heavens Johney is that you?" shrieked Katherine, springing to the door and opening it, as she recognized the voice of the Swedenberger.

"Thank God they are not all dead," ejaculated the old man as entered the little building followed by fifteen or twenty of the settlers at Mansfield. In a few moments the little room was lighted and such assistance afforded to the hungry, exhausted, and wounded inmates as their respective conditions required.

"I was certain you were killed, or taken prisoner," said Die to the Swedenberger.

"I was taken prisoner, but found it convenient to escape."

"How did you effect your escape?"

"I never remain a prisoner long" returned he "when there is but one life between liberty and bondage. I got off by the sacrifice of but one life, in which I was justified, for the safety of many depended on my escape."

"Well, you have saved us, and may heaven reward you," returned Katherine, taking the old man's hand in hers.

"No Catherine, the Indians I presume left as soon as it was dark enough for them to steal away their dead from the door, for we met them several miles from here."

"And they did not attack you?"

"No, I suppose they had fight enough or thought we were more than their really was, for they would expect a reinforcement when they found out that I had escaped from the lad they set to watch me. When we came in hearing of them, we raised the shout, and they seemed as anxious to keep away from us as we were to keep from them."

And thus ends another tale of blood which is yet fresh in the memories of the pioneers of Richland County.

Chapter Seven

Salathiel

In November 1871, Johnny Appleseed was yanked out his stomping grounds in Ohio and later Indiana and introduced to the whole country—in a very popular national magazine, *Harper's Monthly*. English native, clergyman, and journalist William D'Arcy Haley, or more commonly known as W.D. Haley, wrote a seven-page illustrated article entitled "Johnny Appleseed – a Pioneer Hero." Most people were delighted in the wider spotlight for their beloved local character, but some were not.

Salathiel C. Coffinberry of Constantine, Michigan, then in his 60s, the author of the 1839 and 1840 stories about Johnny, was quick to read the magazine and quick to respond on November 23, 1871. He very probably had not written about Appleseed since 1840, when he lived in Mansfield, but he was moved to re-establish the claim of Richland Countians with what he remembered—or was told. He had known Johnny Appleseed and wanted to set the record straight.

As stated before, all transcriptions in this book are verbatim as originally printed, including mistakes and archaic words and usages. Nothing has been changed.

Editor, Shield and Banner:

I noticed in a late issue of your paper a re-publication of the article which appeared in the Nov. number of Harper's Monthly, entitled Johnny Appleseed. This article, being incorrect in many particulars, and inadequate to present the true character of a man with whom I was acquainted from my earliest recollection until I attained the age of manhood, I feel that it is due to his memory to correct these errors, and to present his character as I understand it, with a few incidents of his life which transpired under my own observation.

Respectfully yours,
S.C. Coffinberry

The pioneers of Western Virginia and of the State of Ohio were familiar with Johnny Appleseed, whose true name was John Chapman, not Jonathan, as stated in a recent article in Harper's Monthly periodical.

He was born in the State of Massachusetts, but, at what period, the writer never knew. As early as 1780, he was seen in the autumn for two or three successive years, along the banks of the Potomac river in Eastern Virginia. He attended the cider mills when the farmers made their cider and picked the apple seeds from the pumice after the cider had been expressed. This occupation procured for him the soubriquet of "Johnny Appleseed." After he had procured a sufficient quantity of seed for his purpose, amounting to about a half a bushel at each visit, he started westward with his sack of seed upon his back, on foot and alone, to cross the Alleghenies, and to penetrate the wilderness west of the mountains, embracing what then was known as "The New Purchase," and which is now the state of Ohio.

Years afterward, when the hardy pioneers from Eastern Virginia and Pennsylvania scaled the Allegheny mountains, and sought homes in the valleys of Ohio, they found the little nurseries of seedling apple trees, at Braddock's field, at Wheeling Creek, the Flats of Grave Creek, Holiday's Cover, and at other places along the Ohio valley.

The eccentric, but ever amiable Chapman was also found here, ready to sell his seedlings to the settlers at a 'fippinny bit' a piece. His habits of life were then as they remained until his decease. He would spend a week or ten days among the white settlers, or borderers, then penetrate to his nurseries on the banks of the Tuscarawas; or, as that river was then called in the language of the aborigines, Na-tus-ta-rawa.

At length the fertile soil of Richland county invited the enterprise and industry farther west. Here were traced the footprints of Johnny Appleseed.

On the banks of the Mohecan creek, at Mansfield, near the present site of the Depot of the Pittsburgh and Chicago Railroad, was found one of his seedling nurseries.

In the early part of the summer of 1819 [1809], the father of the writer drove the first team into the town of Mansfield. A party consisting of himself and family, Capt. James Hedges (afterward known as General Hedges) John C. Gilkison, Thomas Lofland, Jacob Newman, Michael Ruffner, Jas. McCleur, Jonathan Oldfield and Johnny Appleseed dined on the public square, near the present site of the old Court House. This was the commencement of the city of Mansfield.

Time! Time! How certain, although slow in thine inexorable fiats!

But three, who were present at that first repast in the city of Mansfield, in the midst of the forest shade, still remain, the writer, who was then six months old, and two older brothers.

For years Johnny Appleseed remained in the vicinity of Mansfield, as his home, or headquarters, from where he would occasionally make trips further west into the wilderness, attend to his nurseries, and return after an absence of two or three weeks.

Near his plantations which were remote from any habitation, he provided comfortable shelters from the inclemency of the weather. Hollow trees and hollow logs, provided with a deep nest of dry leaves served these purposes, in some cases. At his nursery in Sandusky township, near the present location of Leesville in Crawford county (then in Richland county), he erected a shelter by rearing large sections of the bark of the elm tree against a large log. Under this he had a home. From this nursery was obtained many of the orchards of Springfield township. The father of the writer [and] Mordecai Bartley, Joseph Welch, Richard Condon, Matthew Curren and Jonathan Beach, went to this nursery in company, spent the night with Johnny, and packed their trees home the next day on horses.

They supped, and broke their fast, the next morning with the recluse. Both meals consisted of mush made of Indian meal, and the culinary utensil of the household consisted of a camp kettle, a plate and a spoon.

The residence of Chapman at Mansfield covered the period of 1812, and several years following it.

During the dangers and alarms of this period, Johnny Appleseed was regarded in the light of a protecting angel.

On the night or the massacre of Seymour's family on the Blackfork, within a few miles of Mansfield, he left the house of Seymour, on foot, and entered Clinton, one mile north of Mount Vernon, which was not then located, by sunrise, passing every house on his way to give the alarm.

Although I was then but a mere child I can remember, as if it were but yesterday, the warning cry of Johnny

Appleseed, as he stood before my father's log cabin door, on that night; the cabin stood where now stands the old North American in the city of Mansfield. I remember the precise language, the clear, loud voice, the deliberate exclamations, and the fearful thrill it worked in my bosom.

"Fly! Fly for your lives! The Indians are murdering and scalping the Seymours and Copuses." These were his words. My father sprang to the door, but the messenger was gone, and midnight silence reigned without.

Many other circumstances incident to the exposed frontier settlements in the danger that tried men souls manifested the cool courage, the discreet foresight and the mature and deliberate judgment, as well as the fidelity, patience and abnegation of the good Johnny Appleseed.

John Chapman was a small man, wiry and thin in habit. His cheeks were hollow; his face and neck dark and skinning from exposure to the weather. His mouth was small; his nose small and turned up quite so much, as apparently to raise his upper lip. His eye were dark and deeply set in his head, but searching and penetrating. His hair was black and straight which he parted down the middle, and permitted to fall about his neck. His hair, withal, was rather thin, fine and glossy. He never wore a full beard, but shaved all clean except a thin roach at the bottom of his throat. His beard was lightly set, sparse and very black. In 1840 when the writer last saw him in Mansfield this was his appearance, and at that time had changed but little, if any in his general appearance, since he first remembered seeing him when the writer was a small boy. The dress of this strange man was unique. The writer here assumed to say he never wore a coffee sack as part of his apparel. He may have worn the off-cast clothing of others; he probably did so. Although often in rags and tatters, and at best in the plain and simple wardrobe he was always clean, and, in his most desolate rags comfortable, and never repulsive. He generally, when the weather would permit wore no clothing on his feet, consequently his feet were dark, hard and horny. He was frequently seen with shirts, pants and a kind of long tailed coat of the tow-linen then much worn by the farmers. The coat was a device of his own ingenuity, and in itself was a curiosity. It consisted of one width of the coarse fabric, which descended from his neck to his heels. It was without collar. In this robe were cut two arm holes into which were placed two straight sleeves. The mother of the writer made it up for him under his immediate direction and supervision.

John Chapman was a regularly constituted Minister of the Church of the New Jerusalem according to the revelations of Emanuel Swedenborg. He was also a constituted Missionary of that faith under the authority of the regular association of that faith in the City of Boston, Mass. The writer has seen and examined his credentials as to the latter of these. He made quite a number of converts in this county; down to a very recent period, there were several Swedenborgian families in Monroe township, whose religious convictions date back to John Chapman's missionary teachings in the wilderness.

This strange man was a beautiful reader and never traveled without several of the Swedenborgian pamplets with him, which he generally carried in his bosom, and which he was ready to produce and read upon request.

He never attempted to preach or to address public audiences. In private consultations, he often became enthusiastic, when he would frequently arise to expound the philosophy of his faith, on such occasions his eyes would flash, his wiry little form would swell, his voice expand and his clear thought burst into a startling inspiration of eloquence, complete and consummate, exalting and beautiful, forcible and replete with chaste figures and argumentative deductions.

His diction was pure and chaste, and his language simple but grammatical. The year of the erection of the old Courthouse in Mansfield, while the blocks of foundation stone and timber lay scattered upon the public square, a wandering street preacher of the name of Paine, a man with a long white beard, who called himself "The Pilgrim," entered the town. After blowing a long thin tin horn which he carried with him, he assembled an audience on the stone and timbers of the Court House, In the course of his sermon, he pointed to where Johnny Appleseed lay upon the ground with his feet resting upon the top of one of stones and exclaimed: 'See you ragged old barefooted sinner and be warned of the path of sin by his example.'

Johnny arose to his feet, folded his hands behind him, under his tow-linen coat, and slowing approached the speaker. As the speaker paused a space, Johnny commenced in this wise: "I presume you thank God that you are not as other men?"

"I thank God that I am not as you are," retorted Paine.

"I am not a hypocrite, nor a generation of vipers. I am a regularly appointed minister, whether you are or not. Lord be merciful to me, a sinner!" said Chapman and walked away.

In 1840 John Chapman made his last visit to Mansfield, at that time he informed the writer that his home was near Fort Wayne in the State of Indiana, and that he had a sister residing near Fort Wayne.

In the character of John Chapman, there was nothing light or frivolous. He was free from all affection. He never affected the style or language of the sacred scriptures. His language was plain, simple and graphic – his manner earnest and impressive. His utterances always commanded respect, and, after often deep and thoughtful consideration from those who heard him. His deportment was uniformly chaste and respectful, and marked by a passive dignity.

In his method of thought he was analytical, and, in his line of argument varying between the inductive and logical. He spoke with ease and apparently without effort in a natural and simple, yet elegant, flow of language, to express a deep current or metaphysical reasoning and ethical thought.

He penetrated his auditors, apparently without intending to do so, and moved them without knowing it. Physically he was indolent and fond of ease. The writer once watched him, undiscovered as he was working in his nursery, near the "Big Bend" in the creek near Mansfield. He lay in the shade of a spreading thorn tree in the centre of his nursery, and there, lying on his side he reached out with his hoe and extirpated such weeds as were within his reach only.

He preferred sleeping upon the floors of the farmers as he said the indulgence in the luxary of soft beds would soon beget a bad habit which he could not hope to indulge in this varied method of living.

This man cherished the kindest feeling towards all living things. His every act and steps of life manifested this attribute as the pervading trait of his nature. He was as tender and innocent as a child and as easily moved to tears by the sorrows of others, or even the sufferings of animals. He had been known to pay the full value of horses in their flesh, take them from their harness and with a blessing, turn them to the luxurious pastures of the wilderness to become their own masters. He was never without money, and frequently furnished the house wives with a pound or two of tea at great expense, at that time, although he held that the indulgence in that aromatic luxury was a dissipation.

He bought six breakfast plates at the store of E. P. Sturges, and upon being asked what use he had for so many plates, he replied that he would save dishwashing by having so many; that by eating his meals upon a plate he need not wash dishes more than once a week.

The truth is, he carried the plates to a poor family near the Spring Mills who a few days before had the misfortune of losing the most of their table furniture by an accident.

John Chapman was a man of noble instincts. He lived the good for the sake of the good. He cherished the pure for the reward it brought him a pure soul, a high life and self approbation.

Long will his name be cherished as a household word, and his memory be treasured as a land mark of virtue and goodness, by the few who remain who measure his kindness and goodness by the benefits of which they were the immediate recipients.

Chapter Eight

History Finally Recognized and Recorded

Although direct memories or fictionalized accounts of Johnny Appleseed may have been printed in Richland County since the "Gottfried" stories in 1839-40, none were found until a young lawyer bought the *Mansfield Herald* in 1855 and began publishing interviews with the people he called the pioneers (or their children). Dead since 1845, Johnny still found his way into those accounts. This was the first time oral stories about Johnny Appleseed, many first-hand, appeared in print that could later be found and reprinted mainly as fact. In other words, it was the beginning of the Johnny Appleseed legend as told by those who lived it or heard it first-hand.

The 1839-40 stories by Salathiel Coffinberry that appeared in the *Richland Jeffersonian* newspaper may also have contributed to the memories of the people who read them and therefore to the people who wrote about these memories. The original pages, because of their scarcity, remained hidden until recovered in 1946 by Richland County historian D. W. Garber.

And there we have the key to Johnny Appleseed's story. Whoever rewrites it in the past or today must rely on earlier writings since none have survived from Johnny himself. So, beyond obvious land records and merchants' log books, biographers pick through various descriptions and decide on their own what is reliable and what is not. Sometimes with little relevant evidence, these writers throw in their own prejudices and conclusions. Sometimes they are downright misinformed or careless. Therefore, the Johnny Appleseed legend at every turn has ample chance of being twisted in its next retelling depending on what was read before it. Conscientious though they may be, writers can cite sources, yet never be quite sure they got it right. They can pile up similar details and determine whether this pile is really fact or just repeated fiction.

In most cases the earlier the writing the better. The earliest discovered so far is from Salathiel Coffinberry in Mansfield. The next is due to Roeliff Brinkerhoff.

Brinkerhoff was not a Richland County native or even a descendant of early settlers. He came to Mansfield as a young man of 22 in 1850 to study law with his "kinsman," Jacob Brinkerhoff, a man most famous for his years in Congress and on the Ohio Supreme Court. Roeliff's interest in history was incontrovertible. He jumped into the beginning of the county historical society, and he later would be listed as one of the founders of the Ohio Historical and Archaeological Society.

He explained in a later speech that the Richland County Historical Society had its beginning in 1856,

> when a few of us met at Hemlock Falls, in Worthington township, and among those present were Dr. William Bushnell, of Mansfield, Dr. James P. Henderson, of

Figure 12. Roeliff Brinkerhoff.

Newville, and the Reverend James F. McGaw of Washington village. Born in 1800, Bushnell was one of the town's early physicians and knew every man, woman, and child among the pioneer families, including Johnny Appleseed.

I was then comparatively a newcomer in the county, but my wife was the grand-daughter of a pioneer, and that fact interested me in pioneer history. I was also the publisher of a newspaper and many of my subscribers were pioneers, so that I had a large acquaintance among them. Before we adjourned that day we formed a definite purpose to attempt the preservation of pioneer history. Of those who attended that meeting, I am alone left to tell the story.

During the next three years, the Rev. McGaw and I gathered a great deal of pioneer history, and I published it week by week in the Mansfield Herald. McGaw wrote up the southern townships and I took up the others, and in that way we secured the facts from pioneers then living.

We were really making a good deal of progress in securing the facts of the early history of the county, when all at once the Civil War came upon us like a tornado, and during the years it lasted there was no room for anything else. However, the war at last came to an end, and the turbulent years that followed quieted down, and finally we were able to remember that Richland county had a pioneer history as well as a war history, and thereupon in the autumn of 1869 a call was issued for a pioneer picnic in connection with the county fair in Mansfield. To this invitation there was a gratifying response, and the result was that a Richland County Pioneer and Historical Society was organized, with the following officers: Alex. C. Welch, of Springfield township, president; Gen. R. Brinkerhoff, secretary, and Henry C. Hedges, recorder. There was a vice president named for each township in the county. With the aid and encouragement of this society, we again proceeded to gather the facts of early history, which were duly written up and published in the columns of the Ohio Liberal, a newspaper published in Mansfield a few years later. At the meeting held in 1869, over two hundred persons were present whose residence in the county antedated 1820. And at that meeting it was resolved that to be entitled to the term of a Richland county pioneer a person must have lived in the county prior to 1820.

Meetings of this society were held in 1876 and 1879. The meeting in 1876 was held July 4th on the public square of Mansfield, and was addressed by Gen. R. Brinkerhoff. This was called the Centennial meeting as that was the Centennial year. The meeting of 1879 was held at the fair grounds, and was also a Fourth of July celebration, and was attended by nearly two thousand people. A number of speeches were made, and the late Rosella Rice gave a paper on the times of the pioneers.

Twenty-three years had now elapsed since the first organized effort was inaugurated to preserve the pioneer history of Richland county, and it was deemed advisable to put into more permanent form the results of research and so all our gatherings of history went into the hands of the publishing firm of A. A. Graham Co., and were concentrated and added to by a nature of things that nothing great or good, or strong in matter or in mind, comes to the earth except it comes through struggle and through storm. It is this law and struggle under it, which has made Ohio, of all the states of the Union, foremost in war and foremost in the councils of the nation.

The original settlers of Richland county have passed away, but to them we of a later generation owe a debt of gratitude which we can only repay by imitating their virtues, and by perpetuating in our children and through them to the generations of the future, the free institutions and the

Christian civilization which they bestowed upon us. With this purpose in view, we have convened this assembly and are glad to welcome our fellow citizens who have accepted our invitation to be present.

The history of Richland County began appearing irregularly in the *Mansfield Herald* on January 21, 1857, and it is not known how many entries came from Brinkerhoff, from reporter McGaw, or directly from readers. Some were signed and some were not. A segment of McGaw's book, *Philip Seymour or Pioneer Life in Richland County* first appeared on September 2, 1857. It dealt naturally with the War of 1812 and has gone through six printings. It still is available today. Its colorful author will be explored in the next chapter.

On August 5, 1857, Brinkerhoff was collecting memories in his newspaper but he was honest about how difficult it was.

> Our experience, thus far, in collecting the early history of Richland, has shown it to be a more difficult task than we had anticipated. Of the early settlers, a greater portion are already in their graves. Some have removed to other States or Counties; and others who have not been particular in noticing the dates and circumstances of events, require time for reflection and examination. Even Township records, from which much could be gathered, are in some instances, missing the first ten or fifteen years. The sources of information, therefore, are not as accessible in all cases as could be desired. There are also in some instances different differences of opinion, in regard to certain incidents of early history, which require to be reconciled.
>
> In view of these difficulties, we have concluded to publish an abstract of what we gather, in patches just as receive it, hoping thereby to excite inquiry and call out further information. After we have thus collected all that we can

get we shall revise, digest and, as a whole, publish it in book form for a permanent record. We trust that all the old citizens will interest themselves in our undertaking, and make it their business to furnish us all the information in their possession. The pioneer history of this county, if written at all must be written soon; at present it exists for the most part, only in the memories of men, whom, in a very few years, at the farthest, must be gathered to their final resting place. We hope therefore, that every assistance will be extended to us in our attempt to gather and preserve these recollections in a more enduring form.

No wonder many of these stories, or memories, were about wild animals—who could argue? Although it does cause you to wonder how John Chapman survived all those years, on foot in the wilderness. It paid him to have friends, with cabins, in more ways than one.

It was in this August 5, 1857, *Mansfield Herald* that Johnny Appleseed was featured in a history of Monroe Township. It is obviously a summary taken from many sources and filtered through the editor, and perhaps a reporter. The dialog probably is improvised. Much of it has survived as part of the Johnny Appleseed legend today.

> Monroe township is noted as being the head quarters of the eccentric "JOHNNY APPLESEED," as distinguished in the early settlement of this county for raising Appletree nurseries.
>
> The following scraps, illustrations of his personal character and history, have been furnished by Mr. James Sirpless, of Washington, Mrs. Hildreth, of Mansfield and others, who were well acquainted with him.
>
> His proper name was Jonathan Chapman, but he was called "JOHNNY APPLESEED" because of his mania for

planting Apple seeds, and rearing trees for the pioneers. On this account he was really one of greatest Benefactors of Richland County, or at an early period, large orchards, the result of his labor, flourished in all parts of the county.

He brought his seed in large quantities from the Ohio river, and selecting a rich loamy spot, near a water source, he cleared it, put in the seed and enclosed the ground securely, visiting the spot from time to time to clear it of weeds.

Several of these nurseries were located in Monroe township, one on the farm now owned by Mr. Michael Hogan, another on Mr, John Oliver's farm near Loudonville, a third near Petersburg, one near the "Big Spring" in Mansfield, and several near the headwaters of the Whetstone.

"Johnny" was always ready with his trees for the settlers as they "cleared up," giving them the trees or receiving in exchange some old coat or needed article for use. He cared not for pay. He had a great mission to fill, a work of love to perform. The apple was the noblest fruit of the clime, and with it the wilderness should be supplied. And as the county became settled his sphere of operations was removed farther west, when the same career of usefulness was re-enacted.

He would often speak of himself as being "a messenger sent into the wilderness to prepare the way for the people, as John the Baptist was sent to prepare the way for the coming of the Savior." So he was sent on a less important mission to herald the news of approaching civilization.

He was a kind of Swedenborgian; he circulated his doctrines among the settlers very industriously, and found many who sympathized in his opinions. He carried around Swedenborg's books and circulated them, and as the demand was often greater than the supply he would take the books to pieces and distribute the parts.

He believed this world to be a type of the next, that in the future world we would have the same physical geography, the same phenomenon of cold and heat, rains and snow; the same occupations in life, the same emotions of love and hate, joy and sadness, etc., etc.

Some of the Lawyers of Mansfield were once rallying him upon his peculiar notions of the employment of the inhabitants of Heaven.

"Mr. Chapman," said one. "What business Lawyers follow in Heaven?"

"The woe pronounced against them prevents their getting to that place."

"Then where will they go?"

"To Hell."

"And what will engage their attention there?"

"Just what engages their attention here," said the Swedenborgian with the greatest gravity, "they will be placed in the filth up to the knees, and will be striving forever to pitch it into each other's faces."

The Lawyers proceeded to question the next witness!

He was very eccentric in his personal appearance as well as his character.

He was a small nervous man, with black sparkling eyes, and a beard and hair which would have been the pride of a Nazarene as he never allowed them to be trimmed or marred and were of enormous length.

His clothing was always old and ragged. He once bought a coffee bag and making holes for the head and arms, he thrust them through, saying it was a good a wamus as he wanted. In his wilderness journeyings he frequently wore a tin pail or kettle on his head, answering the double purpose of hat and mush pot.

He went barefoot Winter and Summer. Mr. Abner Davis of Worthington township, remembers his calling at his house one cold winter morning when the snow was several inches deep on the ground. He invited him to warm himself by the fire, but he refused and taking his seat in the back part of the room threw his feet up against the logs of the cabin as if he was enjoying the greatest comfort imaginable. The skin of his feet in time came to look much like an elephant's hide.

His diet was very simple. He would not touch tobacco, nor tea, nor coffee, because, when he got to the next world he could not have them there, and he would not cultivate an appetite here which could not be gratified there. Of milk and honey he was very fond and indulged freely, saying he, "we read that this is heavenly food."

He could never be persuaded to marry. He said a spiritual visitor had assured him that two wives were already provided for him in the next world provided he lived single in this.

In 1812 he rescued a beautiful little girl 9 or 10 years of age from death by the Indians near Mt. Vernon, and carried her upon his back many a weary mile until he restored her to friends. From that time forth he had an ardent affection for girls of that age, and said that if he ever married, he would take a girl 8 or 10 years, a pure, beautiful virgin, such as he rescued from the Indians, and train her under his own care until she was a fitting age. Then he would be sure of her purity – he would never marry any other.

Johnny Appleseed was a man of very tender feelings, and could not bear to see even an insect suffer. If he found a bee tree, he always examined to see if the bees had an abundant store from which to spare him a portion for his meal. If they had not, he never touched the comb.

Many anecdotes are told showing his eccentric character.

It is said that one cool night in Autumn, while lying before his Camp fire in the woods, he discovered that the light of the fire attracted the musquitoes and some other night insects, and coming in contact with the blaze were destroyed. This was too much, his feeling were highly wrought upon; and rising from his bed extinguished the flames, remarking that such a destruction of life, in a horrible manner, was too bad – "God forbid," continued he, "that my comfort should be attained by the destruction of any of his creatures."

On another occasion, he made his camp fire before the entrance of a hollow log, in which he intended to spend the night, but on examination he found it inhabited. A she bear and her cubs had already taken a squatter's right, and Johnny believing in the doctrine of squatter sovereignty, relinquished his right, extinguished his fire, and located his claim at the other end of the log. He slept on the snow in the open air, till morning, when returning to the other end of the log, he found his neighbor of the "shaggy coat," comfortably sheltered, giving suck to her children. "Poor innocent things," exclaimed Johnny, "I am glad I did not turn you out of your house."

Another anecdote is related of Johnny, the circumstances of which took place in the public square in Mansfield in an early day.

An itinerant preacher, had made an appointment, to preach there on a certain day, and among the number of his hearers was Johnny. The preacher in holding forth against prevailing fashions and luxuries, exclaimed in a raised tone of voice – "But where now is the barefooted Christian on his road to heaven?" – Johnny who was lying on his back on some timber, taking the question literally, kicked up his heels and bawled out at the top of his voice – *"here he is!"*

One morning while mowing upon the Prairie, he was bitten by a rattlesnake. He involuntarily struck it and left. About an hour after, he recollected the circumstances, and for fear that he might have killed it and the snake writhing in torture, he went back to kill it, if there was no prospect of its recovering from its wound. A friend inquiring of him afterwards about the matter, he drew a long sigh and replied, "Poor fellow! He only just touched me, when I, in an ungodly passion put the heel of my scythe on him, and when I went back, there lay the poor fellow dead."

Such was Johnny Appleseed, the eccentric Swedenborgian. There is not probably, in the history of Ohio, another person combining the same traits of character.

Besides the raising of apple tree nurseries, Johnny was extremely engaged in sowing the seeds of many wild vegetables, which he supposed possessed medicinal properties, such as dog-fennel, penny royal, may apple, hoarhound, catnip, wintergreen, &c. &c. His object in doing this was to equalize the distribution, so that every locality would possess a variety. Johnny was decidedly a Botanical Physician.

[We hope all Persons in the Country, acquainted with facts in Johnny's history, will furnish us with them speedily]

Other anecdotes about Johnny Appleseed are sprinkled throughout pioneer stories in the 1857 and 1858 newspapers. This effort to record settlers' memories eventually resulted in a book, greatly expanded, *The History of Richland County*, compiled by A.A. Graham in 1880.

While Richland County pioneers told Brinkerhoff in the pages of the *Mansfield Herald* about many other aspects of early settlement, two authors associated with this project stood out, James McGaw and Rosella Rice. Their stories follow.

Chapter Nine

A Glorified Pioneer History

James McGaw was one of Richland County's storytellers that without doubt popularized Johnny Appleseed and prolonged his reputation, even though almost from the very beginning it was said his book *Philip Seymour: A Pioneer History of Richland County* was a highly romanticized version of local history. It resulted from his interviewing quite a few pioneers and listening to quite a few tall tales, and stirring in some his own colorful imagination.

However, some took it quite seriously, and McGaw's version of pioneer Richland County, and Johnny Appleseed, easily became all mixed up with the truth.

A native of Pennsylvania, he moved in 1854 with his family to Washington Township, Richland County. Born in 1823, he was a teacher and a Presbyterian minister, like his father. He must have jumped right into the history of Richland County, because he was recorded as attending the first historical society meeting in 1856 at Hemlock Falls.

He was also an author of two other books, *The Thrilling Narrative of Samuel Brown's Horrible Sufferings and Miraculous Escape*, in 1852, and *The Impressed Seaman: Life on Board a British Man of War*, published later in 1857 in Mansfield.

According to Roeliff Brinkerhoff, also a founder of the historical society and at this time the editor of the *Mansfield Herald*, McGaw came up with the idea of writing for the paper a history of Washington Township. After traveling throughout southern Richland County, McGaw expanded his efforts to Mifflin, Monroe, Jefferson, and Worthington townships.

He reportedly gathered his information from the pioneers themselves, a motley crew, and Brinkerhoff wrote in his memoirs "We are all indebted for the preservation of many items of early history, which otherwise would now be entirely out of reach."

Using the old form of McGaw's surname, Brinkerhoff also wrote in the *Mansfield Herald* on June 3, 1857:

> Rev. James M'Gaw is traveling through the county gathering material to write the history of the different townships in the county. This is a work in which all are interested, and we trust every facility will be furnished him for bringing out a work which will be of great interest and permanent value. There are a great many facts in connection with our early settlements, which as yet are only recorded in the memory of the "oldest inhabitant" and before he died it is important that they find a more durable tablet.
>
> We will just say in this connection that Mr. M'Gaw will give frequent lectures on various topics of interest and that he will be found able, eloquent, and a master of his subject.

McGaw also, Brinkhoff wrote, was happy to collect new subscriptions to the *Mansfield Herald*. He must have been a fast writer as well because the first installment on Monroe Township appeared in the paper on August 5 under the state-certified (pre-copyright) heading "Local History, Richland County" and morphed into "History of Richland County by R. Brinkerhoff and Rev. J.F. McGaw." The columns appeared sporadically, sprinkled with Johnny Appleseed material, until the end of 1858.

Out of these stories grew McGaw's book. The first installment appeared on September 9, 1857. It was said to be wildly popular and sold a lot of newspapers. Naturally, it was about the War of 1812 in Richland County, "massacres" and all. Later it was published in sections, then as a book several times through 1909, sometimes with comments at the end by local historians. It has been republished and is available today.

When the book appeared as a listing in the weighty *Ohio Authors and their Books* in 1962, there was another hint on the origins of McGaw's story. Brinkerhoff's *Mansfield Herald* was the successor in 1850 to the *Richland Jeffersonian*. Bookseller Ernest J. Wessen, who had sold the rare *Richland Jeffersonians* in 1946 to historian D. W. Garber, was a major contributor to this book.

He is not credited, but by 1962 it was assumed by somebody that Brinkerhoff also inherited all the old *Jeffersonian* copies; and it was there that he, or McGaw, discovered the 1839 and 1840 stories by "an anonymous author" (Salathiel Coffinberry).

The 1962 reference book said:

> It was upon this framework that M'Gaw draped in fictional form the result of his several years of research. In other words McGaw's *Philip Seymour* was based on Coffinberry's "The Massacre" and "The Battle."
>
> The book [McGaw's] provides the most authentic source on one of the most colorful episodes in the frontier history of north central Ohio.

Although the book was accurate in many details, *Philip Seymour* is now considered to contain a great deal of fiction—exciting, interesting but fiction. Maybe it always has been such. First of all, Seymour was the anglicized version of Zeimer or Zimmer which appeared on their tombstones.

McGaw stirred in plenty of romance, making up out of whole cloth Katharine Seymour's lover, Henry Monroe, as well as the beautiful adopted daughter, Lily, of the Indian Chief Captain Pipe. She ended up being the captured, but unrecognized sister of another friend and was white, not Indian. Although Captain Pipe had lived toward the end of his life in nearby Jeromestown, he never was associated with the War of 1812 attacks.

The snakes and wolves in other chapters were probably as accurate as the pioneers could make them.

Johnny played a big part in *Philip Seymour*, but was not the central character, mostly often passing and speaking in the woods. He was not at the attacks in this version, and his name this time was Appleseed, not The Swedenberger. Much of what was then told about him—tin pot for a hat and bare feet—were already familiar. He talked grandly of his beliefs. He was presented sympathetically as a friend and helper, during this time, of the white settlers. He was called old, as Coffinberry had, even at 37.

At the end of the book, after the Battle of the Thames (October 5, 1813), where Tecumseh was killed, Johnny appears again and says, in part, to Seymour:

> On hearing of the outrage on the Black Fork I repaired thither immediately. I was in Mt. Vernon at the time the murder of your friends occurred. The news of this transaction produced a high state of excitement among the whites. Spies were sent out in all directions to watch the movements of the savages.
>
> On reaching the settlement, I found every cabin tenantless, and on calling at the Block House at Beam's Mill, I found that most of the families had taken refuge there. ... No one could give me any satisfactory account of you after the burial of your friends; no one had seen you since. I then left the Block House and repaired to the scene of the murder,

with feelings of most bitter anguish; and I gazed at your father's cabin (where but a few weeks ago, all was peace and happiness) and saw the work of the destroyer.

It was written he then went to Mansfield, where there was much commotion, and then returned to Mt. Vernon until the spring of 1813 when he tended to his nurseries. Not exactly the stories Coffinberry told, but perhaps closer to pioneer memories.

Since he was so successful with *Philip Seymour*, McGaw immediately published in the *Mansfield Herald* another serial, "Mary Worthington," that he said was based on local happenings. It did not seem to interest local readers.

McGaw soon moved to Indiana—sound familiar?—where he earned a living as a teacher and lecturer. There is no evidence that he wrote books again, certainly not about Johnny Appleseed, who because of the continual reprinting of *Philip Seymour* had landed quite firmly, if not accurately, in history.

Chapter Ten

Rosella Rice Stories

One other budding author answered editor Roeliff Brinkerhoff's 1857 request for historic stories in the *Mansfield Herald*. Actually she may have been well known already around Mansfield and Ashland for her earlier newspaper contributions, prose, poetry, and household tips.

Rosella Rice was not introduced in the paper by name, since pseudonyms were popular then, but as an "accomplished lady of Green Township, Ashland County, Ohio, for the following additional particulars in the history of Johnny Appleseed, together with several very interesting pioneer incidents. We shall hope to receive further communications from the same source." Johnny Appleseed and pioneer incidents would become her specialties in her writing career.

Figure 13. Rosella Rice.

When Rosella Rice was born in 1827 near Perrysville, then Richland County, Ohio, she was the third generation of her family to live beside John Chapman, who would be known as Johnny Appleseed. He was never known to call himself that, even though the name was free advertising for his job of planting and selling apple seedlings to the pioneers.

She called him Uncle Johnny and knew him for the first 18 years of her life. Later as a nationally known author she wrote about these encounters with lots of personal details, not at all from second and third-hand accounts, although there also were these stories she had learned from her family and neighbors.

She would later claim that Johnny stayed at her family's abandoned log cabin on their property when in the neighborhood and that his half-sister Persis Chapman Broom; her husband, William; and their daughters lived on a neighboring farm. She never said when they arrived but that they later moved to Mansfield and then to the Fort Wayne area with Johnny. He loved his nieces, Rosella wrote, but tolerated the idiosyncrasies and shortcomings of his sister and brother-in-law. Stories indicate they depended on him and not he on them.

She wrote about her father helping the Brooms pack up and move to Mansfield, giving them provisions, including a few dollars and building a sled to put them in. The next time Johnny came by, he insisted on giving Alexander back the money. Rice refused.

Rosella grew up to be very sympathetic to Uncle Johnny, as she was to all pioneers, and indeed her grandfather, Ebenezer Rice, and John Chapman were born nearly at the same time, Ebenezer in 1773 and John in 1774, and in the same place. The shared home state of Massachusetts might have drawn them together.

Rosella never knew her grandfather since he died near Perrysville in 1821, although scraps of his life still survive in the Rice papers including

Figure 14. Alexander Rice.

a farm ledger which reportedly included a bill of sale for apple seedlings from John Chapman. It was later clipped out but made a well-publicized circuit of the area for many years.

There is no suggestion anywhere that the families were related, although later in the 19th century Rosella was researching not only her own genealogy but that of the Chapmans'. She also was making notes on the Cooleys, the family of John's stepmother Lucy, and found the Rices and Cooleys had served in some of the same military companies.

Her first magazine article appeared in print in the *Ohio Cultivator* in 1845, the year Johnny died. She was prolific during the height of her career in the 1870s and, when death claimed her in 1888, she was still working on a Chapman genealogy.

Rosella Rice's unsigned newspaper story:

MANSFIELD HERALD, September 16, 1857

Monroe Township – Continued

Johnny Appleseed

Johnny Chapman was born in Boston in 1775

If he entered a house and was weary, he always laid down on the floor with his knapsack under his head for a pillow. The general thing he inquired of the inmates, "Would you like some fresh news, right from Heaven?" and then from his budget carefully unrolled his little, worn, greasy books. One of them a Testament, and the others exponents of the beautiful religion that Johnny lived. The Swedeborgian doctrine, sneered at though it is, if honestly *lived out* cannot fail to make its possessor better and purer hearted, and their lives useful and beautiful. Johnny was never known to injure anything that had life. If he trod upon a worm, or a bee, accidentally, he took it up carefully and grieved over it, saying, "I have taken a life that God has given." What an example for the fast young men of our day, who wantonly kill squirrels and birds and innocent little rabbits!

Johnny thought one time he could do his own cooking on an easier plan than he had been accustomed to. So one morning he got up in fine spirits over his new idea, and going to the sugar camp, he got a little wooden trough from under one of the trees, and filled it half full of corn meal well salted, over this he poured boiling water, stirred it up, and waited until it cooled. He tasted it from a little pine paddle and with a dry chuckle he uttered, "Ugh! I'd rather eat elm bark for breakfast."

It is generally supposed that Johnny had been crossed in love in his younger days. He always talked freely on the subject of love and marriage. He used frequently, if he saw a bright little girl of eight or ten summers, to say he did wish she was his, until he could bring her up to womanhood fair and pure, and unstained by the follies of the world, and with a love all his own.

At one time he took a liking to a blind girl, and intended marrying her in a year or two, if in that time her conduct pleased him. He obtained a good teacher for her, clothed her well, and his poor, old chilled heart grew warm again towards the fairer portion of humankind. But when in one of his journeys, he called to see her, he found her sitting beside a young man in fine spirits and chatting merrily. "She didn't care a snap," he said, "for the poor old man, or she couldn't have been so happy while he was away, weary and toiling just for her," and his voice swelled like a tempest, and his small blue eyes seemed ablaze with anger, as he raised his hand and said – "There is no constancy in woman." I was a little girl then, and crept close up to my mother in fear, while his voice rose and fell in denunciation against the fickleness of the female sex.

Johnny was eloquent and strangely poetical. In discoursing of good fruits, his eyes would sparkle and his face grown animated, and if he was at the table, his knife and fork would be idle and forgotten in the interesting theme. If he was describing apples, we could see them just as he, the word painter, pictured them -- large, lush, creamy tinted ones or rich, fragrant and yellow, with a peachy tint on the sunshiny side, or crimson red, with the cool juice ready to burst out through the tender rind.

Johnny had one sister we know of – Persia Broom, now of Indiana. She was not at all like Johnny. Her husband was the first male child born in Marietta.

Poor Johnny! with all his eccentricities seemed to have had a yearning for home, wife, children and the domestic joys that circle around the family hearth.

His life journey was a lonely one – there were no eyes to brighten at his coming, no warm little arms to fold around his neck – no kisses or smiles or sweet words for Johnny; he was a wanderer going about doing good all up and down our beautiful valleys and hillsides, sowing seeds that would ripen and bless generations that were to come.

D.W. Garber and Rosella Rice

D. W. Garber in the 1960s produced many revised versions of his unpublished Appleseed biography; however, one chapter was never revised, the one on Rosella Rice.

This reflects Garber's devotion to Rice's work and his contention that she was most instrumental in establishing Appleseed, both reality and reputation, in America's host of folk heroes. She also went nameless or ignored in many subsequent biographies because she was a woman considered "romantic," unheralded and thus worthless by many who never read the enormous extent of her writings. Thus, Garber's very extensive local research on Johnny Appleseed was also an extensive project in the 1960s on Rosella Rice. When she died in 1888 she left lots of published stories in magazines and newspapers and unpublished manuscripts among her descendants, who hoarded what they could. Thus, history was saved, and Garber duly reported it.

He no doubt heard about her, since he was born and raised in the tiny Richland County town of Butler, just a few streets over from where her daughter, Lily Rice Stahl, lived until her death in 1943. The two oldest grandsons, Francis and Russell, were a bit older than he, but Garber may have gone to school or played stick ball with the youngest, Wilbur, who was about a year younger.

Here, finally, is his unchanged chapter on Rosella Rice, along with more extensive examples of her Johnny Appleseed work, because it was not considered relevant in its revealing details by his editors. Just as she was devoted to telling the story of Richland County pioneers, she was determined also to tell the story of John Chapman, or Johnny Appleseed, and Garber years later was eager to help.

Garber's Rosella Rice chapter:

> Bernard DeVoto [a well-known 1950s biographer] once wrote that "biography cannot simplify, and must not omit." Based on this premise any attempt to write about John Chapman must include recognition for Rosella Rice. She was one of the first to write about him as Johnny Appleseed, and subsequent writers, either knowingly or unknowingly, have used her material.
>
> DeVoto also commented that "Literary people should not be permitted to write biography," and this, perhaps is a reasonable explanation for the criticisms leveled at Miss Rice because she was a romantic writer. She was a romanticist, but without her contribution much less would be known

about Johnny Appleseed, and the story would lack much of its color.

Rosella was a remarkable woman who has suffered the injustice of neglect. She was one of Ohio's most prolific writers, with hundreds of articles appearing in magazines and newspapers over a period of 40 years. The fact that she authored only one book, an autobiographical novel, *Mabel, or Heart Histories* may account for the fact that little is known about her.

Her articles appeared under more than one dozen pseudonyms, and the use of so many pen names has seldom been equaled. For many years she had three, and sometimes four stories in each issue of *Arthur's Illustrated Home Magazine*, one under her own name, the others under her pseudonyms. Often there would be a poem under yet another pen name.

Her first critical recognition was received for her poetry. A comment in Coggeshall's The Poets and Poetry of the West reads: "Miss Rice is a born poet...." and "her prose writings always attract attention and secure a wide circulation, from their peculiar vigor and directness."

Miss Rice did attract attention, and many babies were named Rosella or Chatty because the mother enjoyed Rosella's stories. Editors welcomed her contributions and in an era when women were supposed to be meek housewives, she made her living with her pen. Many years she saved enough from her earnings to make a trip to New England, or some other point of interest, and wrote about her travels.

Upon the death of her friend, T.S. Arthur, she recalled that she had written for him for 33 years. She began writing in 1845, at the age of 18, the year Johnny Appleseed died, and continued until her death in 1888. To try to estimate the total number of articles and stories she authored would be impossible.

Rosella Rice was a romanticist at a time when saccharine was the accepted form of expression for lady writers. The word, however, does not adequately describe the author, although biographers of Johnny Appleseed have stressed the point, presumably with the mistaken belief that because of romanticism her writings lacked both logic and accuracy. This warmth in her personality gave her a feeling and understanding about his peculiarities which enabled her to write concerning him with great perception and appreciation.

There was also a difference, for Rosella's writings were not confined to romantic stories. She was accepted as a respected historian who wrote discriminating articles with thoughtful interpretations. Her powers of observation were keen, and she wrote with a clarity that left little doubt concerning the breadth of her knowledge.

Henry Howe, Horace S. Knapp, and George W. Hill deplored having to sift facts from fiction in their historical researches, but they solicited and accepted Miss Rice's contributions without question. In "Fifty Years Ago, or Cabins in the West," one of the many years of articles which she wrote, she brought to light such characters as Johnny Appleseed; Reason Brody of the Mohican Outlaws; Sally Williams, the half-breed squaw of Chief Journeycake; and counterfeiters who were once active on the forks of the Mohican. Many facts of history she recorded cannot be found elsewhere.

Some of her stories about John Chapman doubtless remain unidentified, buried in magazine and newspaper files. She wrote many of them. Admittedly there were repetitions, but each contained items of information which were not found in those previously published., Her obituary, written by [a cousin and also a historian] Nancy L. Eddy, contained the statement that Rosella was writing a biography of Johnny Appleseed at the time of her death. Unfortunately her papers and scrapbooks were scattered, and any notes she may have left concerning Johnny are lost.

Not only was Miss Rice an early writer about Chapman, but also her description of Johnny was used by the artist for the sketch of the eccentric character which appears as the frontispiece in Knapp's History of Ashland County.

It was also at her suggestion that Johnny Appleseed's name was engraved on a monument, erected in 1882 as a memorial to the Copus family, in recognition of his contributions to the pioneer community. Since Rosella's death, he has been memorialized in many places, but this was the first lasting memorial to his memory.

Rosella Rice contributed more to the legends of Johnny Appleseed and preserved more factual information about him than any other writer. Howe, McGaw, Knapp, Hill, Haley, and others used her material and spread her impressions. She deserves greater credit than she has received for her contributions.

More of Rosella Rice's Work

With all her work and accomplishments, Rosella Rice died too young in 1888 to finish the Chapman biography or perhaps genealogy that she was working on for the state's centennial in 1903. She wrote that she had contacted descendants of Chapman's half brothers and sisters and was frustrated that few were interested and that little was saved, especially in writing.

Then there was the chilling story from Rosella's relatives and neighbors that her attic was full of paper, possibly from or about John Chapman, perhaps just old magazines. Long after she died and the Perrysville house changed hands, they said these papers were tossed from the attic to a bonfire in the backyard.

This is hard to believe since so much of her letters and manuscripts, as well as her writings published in newspapers and magazines, had been carefully collected and saved by members of her family. Several generations of the Rice family papers have been donated to and sold to the Butler, Ohio, and Clear Fork Valley Historical Society. These include stories, both printed and in manuscript, about John Chapman. Only one original letter written in 1880 survives from a Chapman relative, Nathaniel Chapman of Chandlersville, Ohio, the son of John's half brother, Nathaniel, the only true evidence that Rosella was in communication with the Chapman family. He was 70 years old when the letter was written and lived until 1900. The letter is printed below as the original is handwritten.

Letter from Nathaniel Chapman III, 1880:

Miss Rosella Rice

I received a letter from you a few days ago, saying you would like to have the reading of the History of the Chapman family. I have not got it in my possession now. I think it can be had. Mrs. Moony of Cardington O. had a copy of it some time ago. She has been written to within a few days past to learn if she will loan it to you. As soon as I hear from her, I will let you know.

I examined the History some years ago, and did not find any trace of my Father's family within said History. Many years ago I was residing at my Father's, and learned that he had received a letter from the Chapman family requesting him to write a history of his Father's family and forward it to them for publication. I suppose he must of neglected to comply with the request. Therefore our family was not represented in said History. If you get said History, you will examine it thoroughly for I may have been mistaken about it, but I think I am right. I will give you the nams of my grandfather and his sons and daughters Nathaniel Chapman sen John Chapman (Jony Appleseed), his oldest son, Nathaniel (my father), Perley, Abner, Jonathan, and Davis. Daughters names Lucy Patty Persis, Mary and Sally or Sarah. My grandfather and his family came from

Massachusetts near Springfield in early times, settled near Marietta O. with exception of John Chapman he embarked in the nursery business in the north eastern and northern parts of Ohio. I aught to have answered your letter sooner, but I have been quite unwell for some time past. You will please therefore excuse me. Also, my heavy hand. My pen is very course and blunt.

    Respectfully,
    Nathaniel Chapman

This does not hint of any long-term correspondence, or even that they knew each other at all. It might have been at the beginning of her serious research. However, Rosella wrote the *Shield and Banner* on January 26, 1881, that a "relative of Johnny Appleseed by marriage" had visited them during a meeting of the Wooster Presbytery in Perrysville.

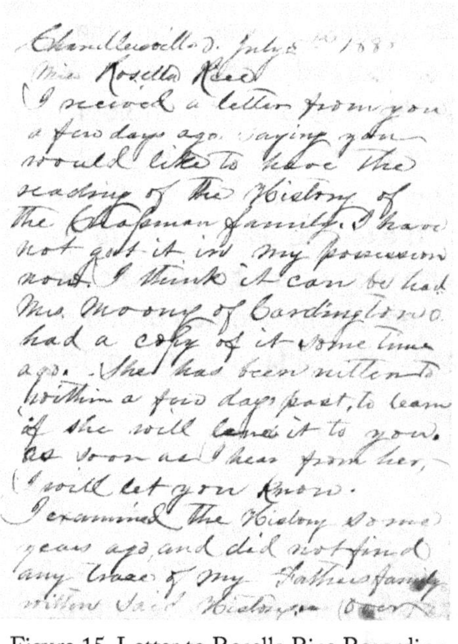

As written, it is unclear whether this was actually Nathaniel, Johnny's nephew, or Nathaniel's son-in-law, but much the same was repeated that was in the earlier letter.

She added, in the newspaper article:

Figure 15. Letter to Rosella Rice Regarding the Chapman Family History.

> We say this, a little vexed in spirit, for we seen now how many interesting items could, with proper and patient search, have been obtained for the late new history of Richland County [1880, Graham]. No doubt Johnny's

relatives are scattered all over Ohio, and if they had been interviewed, could have helped to make the brief account concerning this old man in whom all are interested, a very readable and charming chapter.

One old man with whom we conversed knew that Johnny had a brother named Jonathan, and another man had seen his brother Davis. His sister Persis Brown [Broom] lived in this vicinity and in the neighborhood of Mansfield for many years before removing to Indiana. We think it is a little strange that none of our old residents can recall anything the garrulous Mrs. Brown [Broom] ever said about any of her brothers and sisters.

Her own family consisted of four daughters, Lucy, Mary, Sarah and Harriet Amanda. Lucy married a man in the vicinity of Mansfield named Johns, and moved to Van Wert or some of the Western counties of the State. Mary worked at Lindley's hotel and married a man who was boarding there by the name of John Herald. Herald was called a fencing master, and adept in the use of the sword, and perhaps he taught the art in Mansfield in 1835-36. He was one of Napoleon's men, was skilled in military tactics, had a very dignified and noble bearing, was a foreigner, his face pitted with small pox, he delighted in martial music and excelled playing a wind instrument. How he came to marry a shy, dark girl, timid even to bashfulness, we often wondered. But he seemed proud of her, and we are sure the Brown [Broom] family were much elated over the connection.

Rosella

Obviously Rosella Rice knew quite a bit about the Chapman family, and she was aggravated over both the accuracy and the extent of what had been set down in print. She probably would have collected and preserved a lot more information about John Chapman if she had not died in 1888 and if some

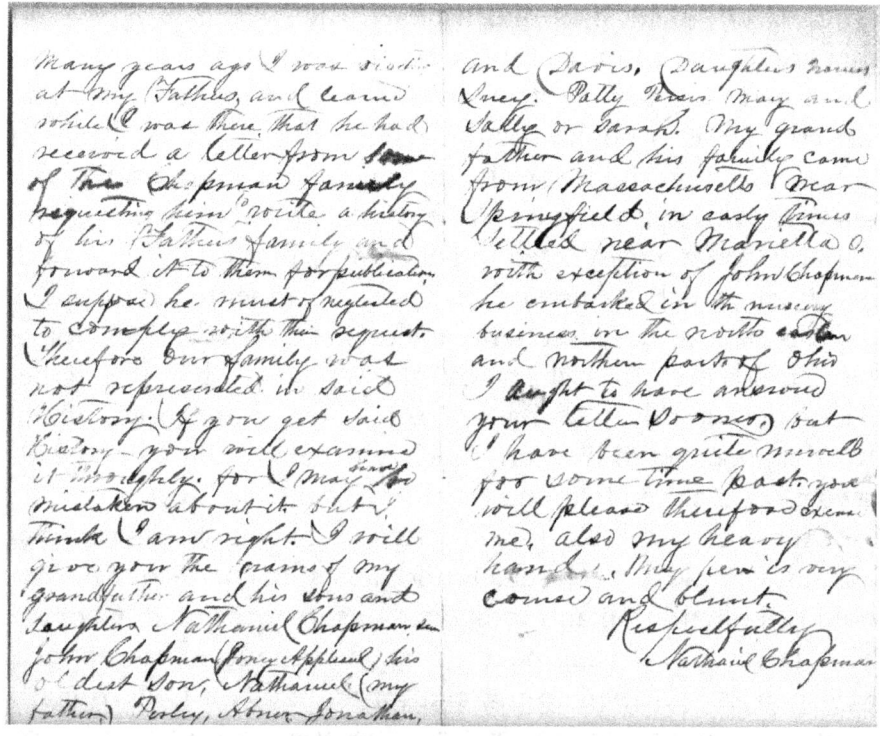

Figure 16. Last Two Pages of the Letter to Rosella.

of her family had not been so eager to destroy what she had already gathered.

Rice was a prolific national author in her day but largely has been ignored. I believe, as did Garber, that she was unfairly dismissed by male biographers of Appleseed, who all drew on her memories and reporting of other people's memories and writing. Her writing has been described as "florid," her details "sentimental," and her stories as "romantic." One actually called her history "unreliable." Actually, reading her newspaper and magazine stories written from 1845 through 1888, reveals her humor, sarcasm, criticism, and careful selection of detail.

She wrote hundreds of stories, and some are quite conversational and deal with people's feelings for each other although not heavily weighted as such, but she also wrote four series of articles, full of facts, for the national *Arthur's Home Magazine* that are a great resource for life on the Ohio frontier.

When Garber first started researching Rice, he wrote and visited dozens of booksellers and found dog-eared examples of her work. More importantly, he sought out descendants and relatives who still retained some of her prized scrapbooks and unpublished works written in pencil on scrap paper. Because of his efforts, much of her work has been documented and copied.

Rosella was the oldest of five children. Her mother Sally Johnson Rice died in 1841 along with the youngest, a boy. Her father Alexander quickly married again, to Mary VanScoyoc, whom Rosella appeared to like very much and called "Our Little Mae." Two more children followed before Mary died in 1854.

Her only sister, Rosina, just two years younger, married at 20 and went west, so Rosella found herself in charge of a household full of children and took over all sorts of womanly chores. She started out writing poetry that she submitted first to local newspapers and then to national ones—tips on how to cook, clean, sew, and make do for less. She drew quite an audience, and even offered to start women's departments in publications. She also applied for a teacher's certificate and was active in education and women's rights.

Luckily she liked children, and in 1854 had her own daughter Lily, although she never married. Everyone, including her descendants, swear the father was never revealed, although some ventured guesses.

She also wrote about Johnny Appleseed for local histories. There is no way, without collecting all her stories from dozens of publications, that anyone can be sure how many times his name was mentioned in her histories. Some articles are repetitive, but others present unique jewels about him that nobody has found before. Her words about Uncle Johnny have been used many times, without credit, by other authors, including W. D. Haley in *Harper's Monthly* in 1871, who received acclaim for introducing Johnny Appleseed to the nation.

Although Haley wrote widely on other subjects, he never was known to write about Johnny Appleseed again. He worked for Ashland County's Loudonville Independent in 1870 and 1871, and therefore borrowed heavily from local accounts. Newspapers around Richland County quickly reprinted his article and it received some criticism from those who claimed to have known Johnny Appleseed personally. This included Salatheil Coffinberry who had written about him as "the Swedenberger" in 1839 but now was practicing law in Michigan and writing about other things.

Rosella continued to write about him. One of her later stories, which seemed to gather up much of what she had already compiled on Johnny Appleseed, added she had traveled to Fort Wayne and was upset that he did not have a proper gravesite with a tombstone. While many letters to her family survive, none do about such a trip. Her grandson, Wilbur C. Stahl told another local researcher in 1943 that she and her daughter, Lily, Wilbur's mother, had visited friends in Fort Wayne in 1884, where they were taken to what was presumed to be Johnny's grave.

In 1882 she had insisted that his name appear on a stone memorial at the site of the 1812 Copus murders, the first memorial to Johnny Appleseed until an obelisk, funded by Martin Bushnell, was erected in 1900 in Mansfield's Middle Park. Some confused his name on the Copus memorial as an indication that he somehow was present at the attacks, but there is no evidence that he was.

Chapter Eleven

More Rosella Rice Stories

Presented here is some of Rosella Rice's work on Johnny Appleseed. The first is transcribed from three loose pages in her handwriting found among her papers. Although the manuscript pages are unnumbered, it is believed to be complete. To make the transcript easier to read, it has been separated into multiple paragraphs.

Johnny Appleseed

Among those whose names stand conspicuous in the memorials of the early settlers is that of John Chapman, but more usually known as Johnny Appleseed. Few were more widely known or more extensively useful to the pioneers that this benevolent and blameless man.

The evil that he did, if any, appears not to have been known; the good that he accomplished was not "interred with his bones" but lives after him. Few men, as unpretending, have been more useful to their race in their day and generation.

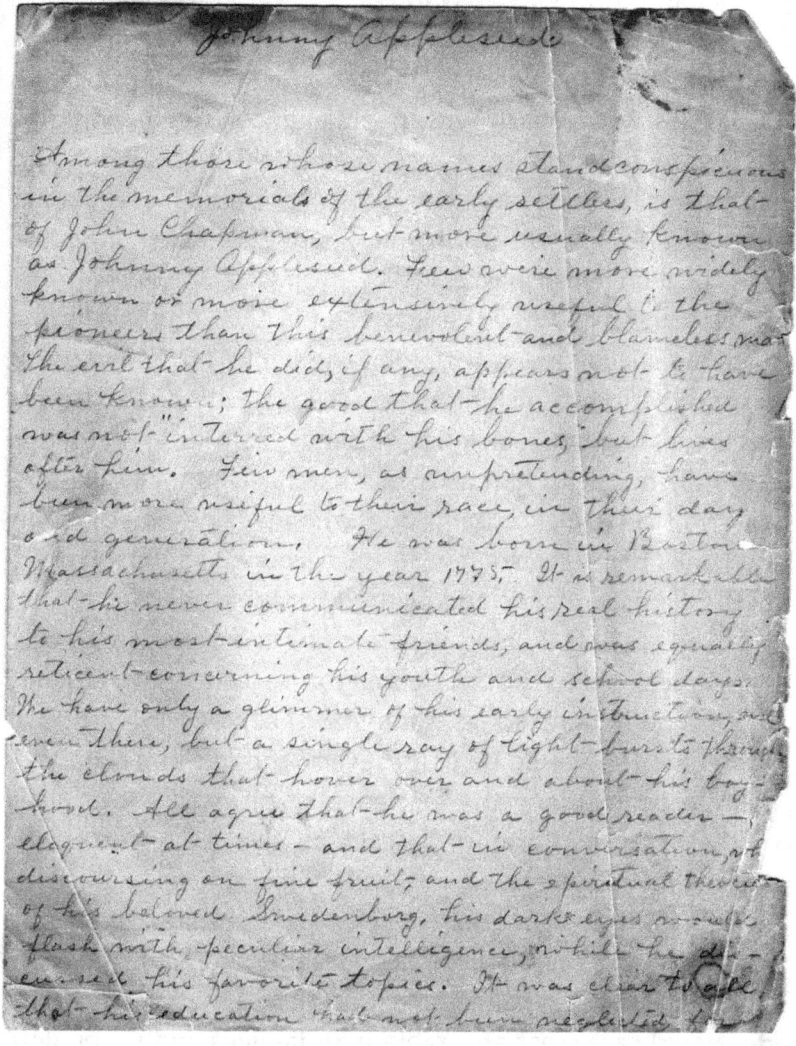

Figure 17. Rosella Rice manuscript.

He was born in Boston, Massachusetts, in the year 1775. It is remarkable that he never communicated his real history to his most intimate friends and was equally reticent concerning his youth and school days. We have only a glimmer of his early instruction and even there but a single ray of light bursts through the clouds that hover over and about his boyhood.

All agree he was a good reader—eloquent at times – and that in conversation, when discoursing on fine fruit, and the spiritual theories of his beloved Swedenborg, his dark eyes would flash with peculiar intelligence, while he discussed his favorite topics. It was clear to all that his education had not been neglected for he possessed a fair fund of information upon many subjects not connected [to] his fruit enterprises.

As early as 1796-7, he was seen in the autumns, in two or three successive years, along the banks of the Potomac, in eastern Virginia, visiting the cider mills where the farmers were pressing cider, picking the seeds from the pumice. He generally had with him an axe, a hatchet and a Virginia hoe, with which he cleared and dug in loamy or rich soil along the banks of a stream a few rods of ground around which he erected a brush fence and planted his apple seeds.

Ever restless, Johnny kept moving from point to point. His nurseries were not neglected for he frequently returned and pruned them so as to make the trees symmetrical. Sometimes he would be gone several months and then suddenly appear among the pioneers, all tattered and bruised by the briars and brambles, ready to give them fresh news – right from Heaven.

His food was generally meager and consisted of berries, nuts, vegetables and a little cornbread or mush made from meal given him exchange for trees or as a matter of charity. He would rarely eat at a table with families and never until he felt sure there would be enough left to satisfy the hunger of the children.

He was well known among the Indian tribes and from his harmless demeanor was regarded as a "great medicine man" and never incurred hate and suspicion of the warriors.

He died at the house of William Worth in Allen County, Indiana, March 11, 1845. Some days prior to his death, information was conveyed to Johnny, who was some fifteen miles distant from Mr. Worth, near where he had a nursery, that some cattle had broken into it, and he immediately started.

When he arrived, he was very much fatigued, having exhausted his strength in the journey, which was being performed without intermission and on foot, was too great a task for the poor old man. He laid down that night, never to rise again, for he was attacked with pneumonia and in a few days he passed into the spirit-land.

He was buried in David Archer's grave yard, two and a half miles north of Ft. Wayne, near the foot of a natural mound and a stone set up to mark the place where he sleeps.

So long as his memory lives will a grateful people say: "He went about doing good."

* * *

Knapp's History of Ashland County, 1863, Chapter IV, p31

Johnny Appleseed.

The accomplished pen of Miss Rosella Rice contributes the following agreeable sketch of the old man:

He was born in Boston, Massachusetts, in the year 1775. No one knows why Johnny was so eccentric. Some people thought he had been crossed in love, and others, that his passion for growing fruit trees and planting orchards in those early and perilous times had absorbed all tender and domestic feelings natural to mankind. An old uncle of ours tells us, the first time he ever saw Johnny was in 1806, in Jefferson County, Ohio. He had two canoes lashed together, and was taking a lot of apple seeds down the Ohio River. About that time he planted sixteen bushels of seeds on one acre of that grand old farm on the Walhonding River, known as the Butler farm.

All up and down the Ohio and Muskingum, and their then wild and pretty tributaries, did poor Johnny glide along, alone, with his rich freight of seeds, stopping here and there to plant nurseries. He always selected rich, secluded spots of ground. One of them we remember now, and even still it is picturesque and beautiful and primal. He cleared the ground himself, a quiet nook over which the tall sycamores reached out their bony arms as if in protection. Those who are nurserymen now, should compare their facilities with those of poor Johnny, going about with a load in a canoe, and, when occasion demanded, a great load on his back. To those who could afford to buy, he always sold on very fair terms; to those who couldn't, he always gave or made some accommodating trade, or took a note payable — some time — and rarely did that time ever come.

Among his many eccentricities was one of bearing pain like an undaunted Indian warrior. He gloried in suffering.

Very often he would thrust pins and needles into his flesh without a tremor or a quiver; and if he had a cut or a sore, the first thing he did was to sear it with a red hot iron, and then treat it as a burn.

He hardly ever wore shoes, except in winter, but if traveling in the summer time and the rough roads hurt his feet, he would wear sandals and a big hat that he made himself out of pasteboard with one side very large and wide and bent down to keep the heat from his face.

No matter how oddly he was dressed or how funny he looked, we children never laughed at him, because our parents all loved and revered him as a good old man, a friend, and a benefactor.

Almost the first thing he would do when he entered a house and was weary was to lie down on the floor, with his knapsack for a pillow and his head toward the light of a door or window, when he would say, "Will you have some fresh news right from Heaven?" and carefully take out his old worn books, a Testament and two or three others, the exponents of the beautiful religion that Johnny so zealously lived out – the Swedenborgian doctrine.

We can hear him read now, just as he did that summer day when we were busy quilting up stairs, and he lay near the door, his voice rising denunciatory and thrilling – strong and loud as the roar of waves and winds, then soft and soothing as the balmy airs that stirred and quivered the morning-glory leaves about his gray head.

His was a strange, deep eloquence at times. His language was good and well chosen, and he was undoubtedly a man of genius.

Sometimes in speaking of fruit, his eyes would sparkle, and his countenance grow animated and really beautiful, and if he was at table his knife and fork would be forgotten. In describing apples, we could see them just as him, the word-painter, pictured them – large, lush, creamy-tinted ones, or rich, fragrant and yellow, with a peach tint on the sunshiny side, or crimson red, with the cool juice ready to burst through the tender rind.

Johnny had one sister, Persis Broom, of Indiana. She was not at all like him; a very ordinary woman, talkative, and free in her frequent "says she's" and "says I's."

He died near Fort Wayne, Indiana, in 1846 or 1848, a stranger among strangers, who kindly cared for him. He died the death of the righteous, calmly and peacefully, and with little suffering or pain.

So long as his memory lives will a grateful people say: "He went about doing good."

* * *

"Reminiscences of John Appleseed" is an obscure clipping from *The Farmer*, in Rosella Rice's scrapbook, no date or origin found. It is from a D. W. Garber copy and not found in the scrapbook donated to the Butler museum.

All the readers of THE FARMER know something of Johnny Appleseed, the old man who planted the first nurseries in the West, sixty-five and seventy years ago.

From the portico where I am sitting now, I can count no less than six of Johnny's old orchards, or the remains of orchards that were once transplanted from his wild-wood nurseries.

The other day a sudden wind storm came whirling up our little bit of picturesque brook-valley, and dashing angrily into our old relic of an orchard, twisted out by the roots the "papa tree," and then turned and left it lying with its white blossomy head prone upon the ground and its heels up in the air.

Father [Alexander Rice] leaned forward with bright eyes and said, "There goes my tree! Oh, remember when that was set out! My daddy [Ebenezer Rice] packed the young trees home on the old gray mare. There was no road cut them, and people had to pack everything on horseback, even the salt from Zanesville, and the meal from the mills at Fredericktown in Knox County and from Shrimplin's and Odell's mills. When he went to set out the trees Betsey and Patty and Orsan [Orson] and Abbie and I followed at his heels and we picked out the ones we wanted and he set them all in the lower corner of the orchard, and they bore our names. Now they are all gone but Orson's tree. He was the first one in the family of children who died, but his tree lived the longest of any.

"The first time we ever saw Johnny was the day my daddy and Solomon Hill bought their trees. They were laying out a road over the Clearfork, and we were all near the bank of the stream when we were startled by a strange sight in the bend of the creek above us. It was Johnny with two canoes lashed together laded with apple seeds. He had on board an old man and his daughter, by the name of Dunstan. They seemed to be traveling somewhere, and Johnny was giving them a lift. That was in 1811, and we early settlers were always glad to see anybody.

"The canoe stopped, and the men spoke to one another, and in a few minutes they had learned they were all from the same State, in New England. Johnny was born in Boston and had immigrated West several years previous. He had lived in Pennsylvania and Eastern Ohio five years at least for John Coulter saw him going down the Ohio River in 1806 with two canoes lashed together and a load of apple seeds on board.

"I was a little shaver then, but I thought there was a good deal of polish in poor Johnny's manner of address and the language he used. My daddy and Mr. Hill were favorably impressed, and the feeling appeared to be mutual.

"I remember that he urged upon them the necessity of having orchards, and offered to let them have trees on such very favorable term that the bargain was made that day.

"The man who was with Johnny, Mr. Dunstan, gave my daddy an ear of corn when they parted; it was of a reddish color, and in all the years in which we raised that kind we called it the "Dunstan corn." Johnny had two or three bushels of Indian meal back in one of canoes, which he gave to daddy for horse feed. It had been wet and was quite spoiled. I presume he carried the meal with him the same us people carried lunch now when they travel. When he would stop he would make mush out of it.

"I remember seeing him undertake to make mush one time, a year or two afterward when he was boarding in our family. He seemed to think that there was an easier and speedier way of making it than to sift it slowly through the fingers, the way my mother did. He asked her would she care if he tried to make some for himself and she assured him that she would not. He took a clean and newly made sugar trough, put a small quantity of meal in it, sprinkled a little salt on it, and then poured on boiling water. My mother pretended that she did not notice him. When it was considered done, Johnny sat down beside his trough with a tin cup of milk ready for his repast. He thrust his spoon into the mush and found dry meal. He tried it again with the same result. With a little 'poh' of contempt and vexation he put on is big hat and walked out, leaving the half cooked mass for the pigs."

While our father was thinking of these incidents of pioneer life we asked him some questions; one was; "Was Johnny ugly about thrusting forward his peculiar views on the subject of religion? did he like to discuss and was he given to long harangues that made the little pioneer babies wish Johnny would get sleepy and go to bed?"

"Not at all," father answered. He was as modest and diffident as a well-bred woman; and that while his was a clearer vision than was ours, and he longed that all others should enjoy and appreciate to 'fresh news right from Heaven,' with the same enthusiasm and exaltation that he did, he never was officious, or bigoted, or made himself obnoxious in the least degree. He was a tender, charitable, lovable man. In some of his traits of character he was almost womanly. Women all liked Johnny. There was a purity in his nature that endeared him to the pioneer mothers. It was sympathetic. Sometimes he would be absent on journeys into other States, perhaps for six months at a time, and when he returned to the log cabin homes he always found a cordial welcome. The frank, sincere faces brightened beautifully as they told their old friend all the particulars of the last quarterly meeting; the weddings; the births, the long webs they had woven; the lots of plums and pumpkins they had dried; the wolf scalps captured; the quantities of columbo and ginseng roots dug and prepared for the market; when the baby cut his first tooth; spoke the first word; or first walked the length of the puncheon floor.

The name of Johnny Appleseed will live in the memories of people of the West of fifty years ago; long after the names are forgotten of those whom the world calls great. Their fame is cold and bare and glittering as an icicle, while his name, simple and odd, is the sweet familiar synonym for kindness and good will, and an unselfish, broad, comprehensive charity, as noble and as far-reaching as any that ever purified the heart of a man consecrated to a good work.

R.R., Perrysville, O.

* * *

Arthur's Home Magazine

The following was written for an 1876 *Arthur's Home Magazine* and probably the most polished and most inclusive of her many articles about Johnny Appleseed.

I said to father yesterday: "I wonder why when I was a very little girl that I called fennel, or May-weed, 'Johnny-weed?' I never did only when I was very small, and none of us do so now."

"Have you forgotten?" he asked. "Don't you remember that it was called 'Johnny-weed' because poor old Johnny Appleseed introduced it into the then-called Western country?"

Really, I had forgotten it; but it all came back to me, and I remembered it well. Johnny-weed! And what a pest it is to the farmer! Well, that was all the evil the poor man left behind him, while the good he did will never die.

Then we began to talk about Johnny, and father became enthusiastic, and I did wish a reporter was sitting in an adjoining room with the door open, because Johnny Appleseed's name is familiar to many old people who would be glad to hear all about him.

He was born in Boston in the year 1775, and his name was John Chapman — not Jonathan, as it is generally called. He was an earnest disciple of the faith taught by Emanuel Swedenborg, and claimed that he had conversations with spirits and angels. In the bosom of his shirt he always carried a Testament and one or two old volumes of Swedenborg's works. These he read daily. He was a man rather above middle stature, wore his hair and beard long, and dressed oddly. He generally wore old clothes that he had taken in exchange for the one commodity in which he dealt — apple-trees. He was known in Ohio among the pioneers as early as 1811. An old uncle of ours, a pioneer in Jefferson county, Ohio, said the first time he ever saw Johnny he was going down the river, 1806, with two canoes lashed together, and well laden with apple-seeds, which he had obtained at the cider-presses of Western Pennsylvania. Sometimes he carried a bag or two of seeds on an old horse; but more frequently he bore them on his back, going from place to place on the wild frontier, clearing a little patch, surrounding it with a rude enclosure, and planting seeds therein. He had little nurseries all through Ohio and Indiana. If a man wanted trees and was not able to pay for them, Johnny took his note, and if the man ever became able, and was willing to pay the debt, he took the money thankfully; but if not, it was well. Sometimes he took a coat, one of which we remember having seen. It was a sky-blue, light, very fine and firm and soft, made in the prevailing Quaker style, with bright silvery-looking buttons on it, two rows, as large at least as silver dollars. Some way the buttonholes were out of sight, hidden by a fold, perhaps. The coat was a choice wedding garment of a wealthy young Quaker, and in time prosperity and its attendant blessings made the young man grow rotund in stature, and the coat did not fit. Then he had loops put on it; and finally he traded it to Johnny for trees; and Johnny's home was at my grandfather's, and by that means the coat came into our family, and hung by the year on a peg up-stairs.

We little Rices used to wear it at our private theatricals. It was good to wear during every performance we had. A pair of deer-skin pantaloons, a bell-crowned hat, the "Johnny coat," an Indian coat trimmed with something strange and always smelling of wigwam smoke, and our mother's camlet cloak, completed our stock of costume. We have made the tails of the Johnny coat flutter like flags in Gilpin's ride and the witch on the broom. Our regret now is that we had not seen the great Centennial year in the dim distance, and saved the rare old coat for the occasion.

I can remember how Johnny looked in his queer clothing-combination suit, the girls of nowdays would call it. He was such a good, kind, generous man, that he thought it was wrong to expend money on clothes to be worn just for the fine appearance; he thought if he was comfortably clad, and in attire that suited the weather, it was sufficient. His head covering was generally a pasteboard hat of his own making, with one broad side to it that he wore next the sunshine to protect his face. He wore it with the wide side of the rim toward the sun. It was a very unsightly object, to be sure, and yet never one of us children ventured to laugh at it. We held Johnny in tender regard. His pantaloons were old, and scant, and short, with some sort of a substitute for "gallows" or suspenders. He never wore a coat except in the winter-time; and his feet were knobby and horny, and frequently bare. Sometimes he wore old shoes; but if he had none, and the rough roads hurt his feet, he substituted sandals instead —rude soles with thong fastenings. The bosom of his shirt was always pulled out loosely, so as to make a kind of pocket or pouch, in which he carried his books. We have seen Johnny frequently wearing an old coffee-sack for a coat, with holes cut in it for his arms.

All the orchards in the white settlements came from the nurseries of Johnny's planting. Even now, after all these years, and though this region of country is densely populated, I can count from my window no less than five orchards, or remains of orchards, that were once trees taken from his nurseries.

Long ago, if he was going a great distance, and carrying a sack of seeds on his back, he had to provide himself with a leather sack, for the dense underbrush, brambles and thorny thickets would have made it unsafe for a coffee-sack.

I remember very distinctly of falling over one of Johnny's well-filled sacks one early morning, immediately after rising. It was not light in the room at the head of the stairs, and he was not there when I went to bed the night before. It seems that he arrived in the night, and for safe-keeping the sack was put up-stairs while he lay beside the kitchen fire. I never saw him sleep in a bed; he preferred to lie on the floor, with his poor old horny feet near the fire. I have often wondered how he carried that sack of seeds. I should think there was at least a bushel and a half in it, and it was so full that instead of being tied and leaving something for a handhold, it was sewed up snugly, and one end was as smooth and tight as the other. It must have been as hard to carry as a box of the same size. I have heard my father say, however, that Johnny always carried a forestick, or any big stick for the fire-place, on his hip, so it may be that it was the way he carried that ungainly burden.

In 1806 he planted sixteen bushels of seeds on an old farm on the Walhonding River, and he planted nurseries in Licking county, Ohio, and Richland county, and had other nurseries farther west. One of his nurseries is near us, and I often go to the secluded spot on the quiet banks of the creek, shut in by sycamore trees, with the sod never broken since the poor old man did it; and when I look up and see the wide, outreaching branches over the place, like outspread arms in loving benediction, I say in a reverent whisper: "Oh, the angels did commune with the good old man whose loving heart prompted him to go about doing good!"

A silent awe steals over me when I stand there, and I involuntarily step softly and speak low. I seem to see the old man breaking the rich, black soil, and laying aside the green sod, where only the violets have grown for many, many years, and as he drops the tiny seeds into the virgin soil, his good will to the poor pioneer goes with every seed, and God's blessing is with the homeless, wifeless, childless, but beloved and venerated wanderer. He was singularly pure and good. I know that now, after all these years, when I recall how the mothers in the neighborhood loved him. When he came to us after a long absence, the wives and mothers would shake hands, and inquire about his health and his affairs, and talk so kindly and affectionately to him, and tell him about the births and deaths, and the baby cutting teeth, or beginning to toddle and talk at nine months; and though he was singular, and his ways not our ways, and his manner of speech not ours, and his thoughts spiritualized and exalted above ours, yet he manifested such a warm and cordial sympathy that he united himself.

I remember once my sick mother was bathing her feet in warm water, and we cried out: "O mamma! mamma! hurry! A man's coming!"

She started to get up, but seeing through the window who it was, she sat still, saying, "Why it's dear old Johnny!" in a voice that showed how glad she was to have him come—as satisfied as if he had been a good woman.

He prescribed for her headache, and his very voice was full of pity and comfort.

Though my mother was very kind, she liked fun — liked to tease big, overgrown boys and make them say funny things, and writhe and twist rather than confess or make a fair answer. I often recall one time that she so far transgressed as to tease Johnny. He was holding the baby on his lap, chirruping to the little fellow, when my mother asked him if he would not be a happier man if he were settled in a home of his own and had a family to love him. He opened his eyes very wide—they were remarkably keen, penetrating, gray eyes, almost black—and replied in a manner, the words of which I cannot repeat, but the moaning was that all women were not what they profess to be, that some of them were deceivers, and a man might not marry the amiable woman that he thought he was getting, after all.

Now we had always heard that Johnny had loved once upon a time, and that his lady love had proven false to him. Then he said one time he saw a poor, friendless little girl who had no one to care for her, and he found a home for her, and sent her to school, and meant to bring her up to suit himself, and when she was old enough he intended to marry her. He clothed her and watched over her; but when she was fifteen years old, he called to see her once unexpectedly, and found her sitting beside a young man, with her hand in his, listening to his silly twaddle.

I peeped over at Johnny while he was telling this, and, young as I was, I saw his eyes grow dark as violets, and the pupils enlarge, and his voice rise up in denunciation, while his nostrils dilated and his thin lips worked with emotion. How angry he grew! He thought the girl was basely ungrateful. After that time she was no protege of his.

He was very fond of little girls, and I think he liked women better than men. He seemed feminine in many of his attributes, and in his likes and dislikes he was decidedly womanly. I often felt badly — indeed they must have been the pangs of jealousy — when I would hear little playmates say: "He asked mother to give me to him to bring up like a lady;" or, 'Johnny said if he could get me for his wife he'd bring me up the right kind of a way."

Now he never asked my mother for the listening, admiring, curious little lady in the bib apron, who stood back out of sight watching the wild play of his impressive features, and wondering how the poor old man came to use such big words, and rejoicing in his rare eloquence.

And yet he must have noticed the homely child, for often he would read to her out of his old books, prefacing the entertainment with: "Don't you want some fresh news right from Heaven?" That was what he always called it.

On the subject of apples he was very charmingly enthusiastic. One would be astonished at his beautiful description of excellent fruit. I saw him once at the table, when I was very small, telling about some apples that were new to us. His description was poetical, the language remarkably well-chosen; it could have been no finer had the whole of Webster's Unabridged, with all its royal vocabulary, been fresh upon his ready tongue. I stood back of my mother's chair, amazed, delighted, bewildered, and vaguely realizing the wonderful powers of true oratory. I felt more than I understood.

He was scrupulously honest. I recall the last time we ever saw his sister, a very ordinary woman, the wife of an easy old gentleman, [Persis and William Broom] and the mother of a family of handsome girls. They had started to move West in the winter season, but could move no farther after they reached our house. To help them along and to get rid of them, my father made a queer little one-horse vehicle on runners, hitched their poor caricature of a beast to it, helped them pack and stow therein their bedding and few movables, gave them a stock of provisions and five dollars, and sent the whole kit on their way rejoicing.

And that was the last we ever saw of our poor neighbors — the pretty little girls with their sunny hair and their laughing brown eyes, the easygoing old man, and the only sister of Johnny's, the spry little woman who always called me "honey."

The next time Johnny came to our house he very promptly laid a two-dollar bill on my father's knee, and shook his head very decidedly when it was handed back; neither would he be prevailed upon to take it again.

He was never known to hurt any animal or to give any living thing pain — not even a snake. One time, when overtaken by night while travelling, he crawled into a hollow log and slept till morning. In the other end of the log was a bear and her cubs. Johnny said he knew the bear would not hurt him and that there was room enough for all.

The Indians all liked him and treated him very kindly. They regarded him, from his habits, as a man above his fellows. He could endure pain like an Indian warrior; could thrust pins into his flesh without a tremor. Indeed, so insensible was he to acute pain that his treatment of a wound or sore was to sear it with a hot iron, and then treat it as a burn.

He ascribed great medicinal virtues to the fennel, which he found, probably, in Pennsylvania. The overwhelming desire to do good and benefit and bless others, induced him to gather a quantity of the seed, which he carried in his pockets, and occasionally scattered along his path in his journeys, especially at the wayside near dwellings. Poor old man! He inflicted upon the farming population a positive evil, when he sought to do good, for the rank fennel, with its pretty but pungent blossom, lines our roadsides, and borders our lanes, and steals into our door-yards, and is a pest only second to the daisy.

The last time we saw Johnny was one summer day when we were quilting up-stairs. A door opened out upon the ground, and he stood his little bundle on the sill and lay down upon the floor, resting his head on the parcel. Then he drew out of his bosom one of his old dingy books and read aloud to us.

That is one of the pictures which will always "hang on memory's wall." We can see the old man lying with his head on the sill, his gray hair falling away from his placid face, his simple attire, his finely-cut features and the little book in his toil-worn hands, while the wreathing morning glory vines, stirred by the summer wind, framed the picture. His voice had the same old charm, and the same fascination held the maiden spellbound that had awed the little child in the years agone. His voice would rise and fall musically and with a fervid and a strange eloquence that was very singular. Something about it reminded me of the music of winds, and waves, and the murmur among the leafy boughs; a something indefinable and very peculiar.

He felt that God had appointed him this mission of love—this hard, rough toil in the wilderness— that this life and this work was His Gospel to preach daily, that to plant apple-trees which would produce orchards for the benefit of generations yet to come, was his appointed work. What a beautiful faith was Johnny's!

In 1838, he resolved to go further on. Civilization was making the wilderness to blossom like the rose, villages were springing up, stage-coaches laden with travelers were common, schools were everywhere, mail facilities were very good, frame and brick houses were taking the places of the humble cabins; and so poor Johnny went around among all his friends and bade them farewell. The little girls he had dandled upon his knees, and presented with beads and gay ribbons, were now mothers and the heads of families. This must have been a sad task for the old man, who was then well stricken in years, and one would have thought that he would have preferred to die among his friends.

He came back two or three times to see us all, in the intervening nine years that he lived; the last time was in the year that he died, 1847.

In the summer of that year, one day, after travelling twenty miles, he entered the house of an acquaintance in Allen County, Indiana, and was, as usual, cordially received. He declined to eat anything except some bread and milk, which he ate sitting on the door-step, occasionally looking out toward the setting sun.

Before bed-time, he read from his little books "fresh news right from Heaven," and at the usual hour for retiring, he lay down upon the floor, as was his invariable custom. In the morning the beautiful light supernal was upon his countenance, the death angel had touched him in the silence and the darkness, and though the dear old man essayed to speak, he was so nearly dead that his tongue refused its office.

The physician came and pronounced him dying, but remarked that he never saw a man so perfectly calm and placid, and he inquired particularly concerning Johnny's religion.

Poor Johnny! I often fear that "no man knoweth of his sepulchre." I was travelling in a coach a few years ago in the county in which he died, and to all my eager inquiries the reply invariably was: "Well, he's buried some place about here, but I'm not certain just where it is." My heart ached with sorrow and anxiety; I was grieved to think the dear old man, to whom we are all indebted, slept in a nameless grave.

The lumbering coach halted at one time, the horses were reined up at the shady roadside, and the driver hailed down respectfully to "the leddy" that there in that wayside nook was once one of Johnny's nurseries. It was a spot we shall never forget. Tall trees environed it, a brook warbled below it, the winding highway beside it was picturesque and lay through an immense reach of wildwood, and the toot of the stage-horn daily broke the silence. All the rows of trees had been removed from the woodland nursery, and it was now only the delightful haunt of bird and bee and squirrel, while the climbing vines ran riot, and the long grass looked as though it draped the sacred graves of beloved ones.

How I did wish that memorable man of pioneer times, that homeless wanderer whose heart was warm with a love so comprehensive, could have his grave there in the beautiful silence in which he wrought his self-denying work so many, many years of his life! Poor Johnny!

His bruised and bleeding feet now walk the gold-paved streets of the New Jerusalem, while we so brokenly and crudely narrate the sketch of his life. A life full of labor, and pain, and unselfishness, humble unto self-abnegation, his memory glowing in our hearts, while his deeds live anew every spring-time in the fragrance of the apple-blossoms he loved so well.

Because so many of Rosella Rice's stories appeared in newspapers, they are very hard today to find and accumulate. Some have been reprinted, and others have not and are always a delight to discover. They also may be in undated handwritten manuscript form; in undated or dated clippings in scrapbooks, with the source only hinted; or they may pop out full, dated and signed in the pages of original or microfilmed newspapers. Some, no doubt are lost.

To The Editor of The Mansfield Herald

The following Rosella Rice article, more of an explanatory letter, was dated April 12, 1887, and is addressed to the Editor of The Mansfield *Herald*. Mary Jane Henney included it in her *Rosella Rice* book, available at the Ashland County Chapter of the Ohio Genealogical Society. Twenty-five years earlier, D. W. Garber also found a copy, undated, of the original, in one of the scrapbooks kept by the Rice family. The apostrophes inserted in the dates were placed there by Rosella and are printed here as they appeared in the paper. It does not indicate whether it was found in the *Herald*, either hard copy or microfilm, or from a manuscript or clipping. Luckily we have a clipping of the printed story from D.W. Garber's papers. It shows how much she loved the original pioneers and Johnny Appleseed, who lived among them.

> We often say of the old pioneer fathers, "there will never be such again," and we mean it. Such courtesy and honesty, and hospitality, and good common sense, and intelligence, will never be all combined together again, in the coming men.
> We recall one evening a few years ago in which we chanced to hear two of these old noblemen talking. They were boys in those days in which Mansfield was in Green Township. One said Pope's essay on man was always his favorite poem, and the other said his was "vital spark of heavenly flame"; and then they repeated the finest lines in that stately, measured old way that they had been taught, or had taught themselves, and we sat back indoors, and listened

to the old men in the twilight out on the porch with nothing to break the stillness by the crickets in the grass and the sleepy twitter of the young birds in the cedar. And we wished with tears that the dear old weary ones had a tithe of the advantages that the young men have now-a-days.

The peaceful thoughts of the old men went a little further, and one said: "Since I came up to full manhood and think away back, it seems to me folks did not appreciate old Johnny Appleseed. He had a better mind than we knew of. I remember one night when he was staying at father's he lay on the floor, he wouldn't go to bed, and he could look right up through the slab-board roof to the blue sky and stars. He lay with his head on his white muslin knapsack and kept turning and turning over."

"Father spoke to him and asked if he wanted anything, and Johnny said if it wouldn't disturb the family he would like to sing awhile, and he lay there and sang his favorite piece over two or three times,

> The spacious firmament on high,
> With all the blue ethereal sky."
> To the tune of 'Star of Bethlehem.'

"He sang well and that old poem has always seemed better to me ever since. There he lay, on his back, his feet drawn up, his hand back under his head, and his head with the long, flowing hair, tilted up on his knapsack, looking out through the tattered roof at the stars. I never think of old Johnny that this does not come up as plain as if it happened yesterday."

Reminiscences like this, coming to use, often made us wish we could find some of Johnny's writing. It would seem, we thought, to be something very real. We enquired of his relatives, but they had destroyed all old letters, notes and due bills, and everything connected with him. But one search was rewarded a few years ago in finding on a leaf in an old account book of our grandfather's these three lines in Johnny's own penmanship.

Mr. Odle, please to let Ebenezer Rice have the hoops. August 25, 1820, John Chapman

The Mr. Odle was Nathan or Thomas O'dell down at O'Dell's Lake. The order was never taken out of the book. Probably there was no paper about the premises except the coarse yellow brown paper in the account book. We

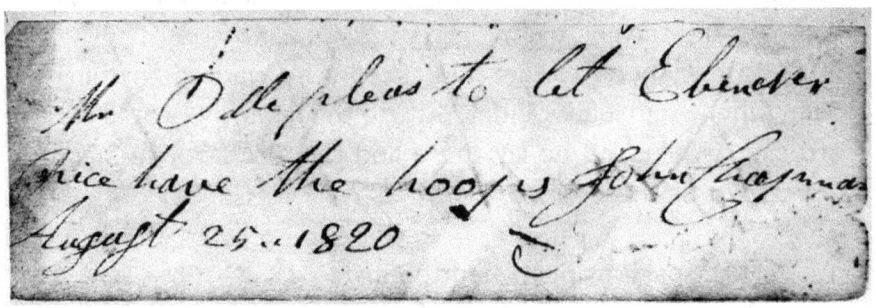

Figure 18. Rare handwritten receipt by John Chapman.

cut the order to put among our store of old-time relics. On the other side of it we find this: "November 15, 18'0, Jacob Beam came to board at my house. (illegible) March 3 (or 5th), Jacob Beam quit shoemaking at my house – 12 days out. Settled Jan. 18'2."

Where Johnny signed his name half the capital C is below the line – like we all make capital J's now days. In referring to the penmanship of seventy and eighty years ago we find the C usually made that way.

Rosella Rice

She plainly loved Johnny Appleseed and managed in these few stories to inject unique details, often having to do with her own family. There are, no doubt, many others, printed and unprinted. If John Chapman, the man, ever had a biographer, it was Rosella Rice.

Chapter Twelve

Dr. William Bushnell

While the earliest writings are often the most valuable, and most honest, do not underestimate the excellent memories of elderly people who claimed to have known Johnny Appleseed very well when asked. The following account from Dr. William Bushnell (1800-1893), a long respected local doctor in Mansfield, is from an interview by independent journalist Henry Stephens. It did not appear in local newspapers, as far as we know. It was sold to various newspapers across the country, this one on August 18, 1888, in the Burlington (Vermont) *Free Press*. Pen-and-ink sketches of Johnny taken from *Phillip Seymour* accompanied the article.

Dr. Bushnell was occasionally the subject of newspaper stories because of his long life, and his memories were used in history books; but he never wrote for newspapers himself. His family, going back to his grandfather, Alexander, was large and contained

Figure 19. Dr. William Bushnell.

many Ohio branches from Trumbull to Richland counties. He was born in Connecticut, and his family, which then included five young siblings, arrived in what is now Ashland County in 1806. The family grew, and William said he, as a boy, accompanied his father, Sterling, in the War of 1812. Among his many accomplishments, he traveled, apprenticed and attended medical school, and served in the Ohio General Assembly.

Apparently, John Chapman was long known and well respected in the Bushnell family. Dr. Bushnell's son, Martin, a Mansfield businessman, paid for the town's first monument, an obelisk, dedicated to Johnny Appleseed in Middle Park in 1900. Another monument was erected in South Park in 1953. What is left of the first is now in the Mansfield Memorial Museum.

The dedication of the original monument prompted Josephine B. Scott of the Maumee Valley Pioneer Association to send Martin Bushnell "a large leather pocketbook" with the Johnny Appleseed autograph written on the inside flap. Hopefully it was signed "John Chapman" since he was never known to sign anything "Johnny Appleseed."

In any case the signature on the purse was supposed to have been authenticated by the Ohio Historical Society. If they kept it, no one knows where the purse is today. Cards remain at the Mansfield Memorial Museum that two leather "bags" were from the estate of

Figure 20. First Johnny Appleseed Monument in Middle Park in Mansfield, Ohio.

Martin Bushnell and belonged to Johnny Appleseed. The bags themselves are missing.

Figure 21. Hon. M.H. Bushnell.

Dr. Bushnell's memories of Johnny Appleseed, when finally they found print—in the following article by Stephens—include a noticeable and understandable lean toward health and medicine. The article includes some well-worn stories and some details not found elsewhere. Remember, however, that this author of Bushnell's account determined what it included. Who knows what would have been told if Bushnell himself had put pen to paper, unedited.

Very little is known about the man who finally caught up with him, Henry Stephens, except that he occasionally is found as author for far-flung newspapers of other history pieces, none involving Johnny Appleseed or William Bushnell.

JOHNNY APPLESEED

A CHAT WITH A MAN WHO KNEW THE PIONEER PROPHET

His Adventure with the Yellow Jacket and His Comic Dress – His Cure for Sore Legs and His Queer Philosophy – His Orchards and How They Were Planted

By Henry Stephens

Mansfield, O., Aug. 9 – "Yes," said Dr. Bushnell. "I knew Johnny Appleseed well, and he was one of the most remarkable characters I have ever met."

These were the words of one of the oldest physicians in the state of Ohio. Dr. Bushnell has long since passed the time which the Bible allots as the natural life of man. His hair is as white as the driven snow, but his step is steady and his mind is clear. He has been for years well known through northern Ohio, and had the honor of being entertained by the king during the international congress of doctors at Sweden some years ago. The king asked the doctor to visit him at his country seat, and he wanted him to prescribe for his wife. He was surprised to find that as old a man would dare to cross the water, and he asked the doctor many questions about this country. I had been chatting with Dr. Bushnell about early days in Ohio, and the conversation turned to Jonathan Chapman, that strange character who was so well noted in western Pennsylvania, Ohio and Indiana during the early days. He brought bags of apple seeds with him and planted orchards all over the west, doing the whole rather as an act of charity than with a view of making money out of his work. He was a philosopher and a preacher, as well as a nurseryman, and he was one of the queerest cranks of pioneer history, said Dr. Bushnell:

"Johnny Appleseed was not, I think, insane, and he was certainly not weak minded. He used to come to my house when he passed through this part of the county. He was a small, wiry man, with thin lips, dark face, and long, dark hair. His eyes were black and sharp and piercing. He had a pleasant smile, but his face was usually sober, and as to his dress, it was as fantastic and dilapidated as you can imagine. It was made up of cast-off garments which he had gotten in exchange for apple trees or seeds, and he cared nothing at all for appearance. I have seen him at times when his chief garment was a coffee sack with a hole at the top for his head to pass through and one at each side for his arms.

"He never wore shoes except in the coldest of weather. He said that shoes hurt his feet, and he could get along better without them. At one time I remember he was at Sandusky on Lake Erie and he wanted to go to Buffalo to the cider mills there for a load of apple seeds. It was in the depth of winter, and the lake was frozen over; he was in his bare feet, and he expected to walk. Some kind-hearted citizens of Sandusky gave him a pair of shoes and forced them upon him. He started out, walking on the Ice. He told me that by the time he had gotten a few miles away from Sandusky, he found his feet very cold, and he concluded it was the shoes that made them so. In order to test it, he took off one shoe, and went with one foot bare. 'I found,' said he, 'that this foot was much warmer than the other, and I then took off the other shoe and threw them both as far as I could throw them. I walked in my bare feet on the Ice to Buffalo, and I got along very comfortably.'

"As to Johnny Appleseed's hat," continued Dr. Bushnell, "he wore anything he could get that would cover his head, and he usually had a pasteboard visor, which he tied over his forehead to shield his eyes from the sun. He usually carried a tin vessel along with him, in which he cooked his mush, and during a part of his life he wore this tin vessel on his head between times as a hat. It was an ordinary tin pan. He was plain in his diet, and his stomach did not trouble him. He preferred vegetable food to animal, and he did not believe in wasting anything. At one time it is said that he took some bread out of a slop bucket at a pioneer's cabin and reproved the woman of the house for wasting God's food."

* * *

He was very kind to animals, was he not?

"Yes, he got his seeds in western Pennsylvania and near Buffalo, and he brought them to Ohio on horses. He would take old, broken-down, cast-off steeds, feed them and drive them along with him to the east. At the cider mills he would soak the mush of the cider, the refuse of the apples in barrels of water and the seeds would fall to the bottom. He would lay them out to dry and when he had gotten about two bushels, he would put them in a bag of leather and load them on one of those broken-down horses. He often carried one of these bags himself under his arm and against his hip and he would often bring several horse loads of them on his western journey. After he was through with the horses, he would turn them loose or give them to some pioneer, urging them to be kind to them.

"As to his own treatment of the animal creation, I have heard him express the greatest regret for having killed a snake, and it is said that he often put out his camp fire at night when it attracted the mosquitoes and flies. It was near here that he had his trouble with a yellow jackets' nest, the story of which has been often told. He was working, I think, at one of his orchards when he stepped upon this colony of yellow jackets. One of them crawled up his pants leg and, although it stung him terribly, he gently forced it down, pressing the cloth onto fully in order that he might not hurt it. He told the bystanders that it would not be right to take the life of the poor thing, as it did not intend to hurt him.

Where did Johnny Appleseed come from?

"I talked with him about his career," replied the white-haired doctor. "He was born, I think, in Massachusetts, and his crankiness came from being crossed in love. He used to refer indirectly to this at times, and he was not particularly fond of the society of women, though he was always respectful to them. It was after he had been jilted by the girl to whom it was said he was engaged that he took to walking about and reading Swedenborgian books, and later on he came westward on his mission. This mission was to circulate the doctrines of Swedenborg and to plant apple trees. He carried his books in a pocket, made by pulling his shirt half way out of his pantaloons, and he stuck these back into this place through the open bosom of his shirt when he was through. He would tear a book to pieces, leaving a fragment at one cabin, another at another, and so on, and he called his books 'fresh news from heaven.' He would often read them aloud, lying down on the floor with his feet toward the fire. I have often offered him a bed when he was here, but he always refused it. He was a good talker, too, and he was nobody's fool."

* * *

Was he a man of culture?

"Well, hardly that, but he had good common sense as to many things, and he undoubtedly did great good. He was something of a doctor in his way, and he had one cure for sores and bruises which he considered infallible. If he bruised or wounded his foot, he would apply a red-hot iron to the afflicted part and thus made a burn which he could heal. I remember a man here who had a very sore leg, the shin of which was broken out in boils, and which he had tried for years to cure. He told Johnny Appleseed of it, and Johnny said he could cure him. He asked to see the sores, and the man rested his leg upon a chair and laid them bare. It was in front of the fireplace, and Johnny snatched up a burning ember and before the man knew what he was about, he had grasped his leg by the ankle and rapidly rolled the red-hot coal over the sores. The man squirmed and yelled, but Johnny held on until he had completed his work. Whether it cured the man I am unable to say.

"Johnny Appleseed," Dr. Bushnell went on, "did not seem to feel pain. I have seen him thrust pins into his legs and arms without quivering. He was a crank on the subject of dog fennel as an ague cure, and he planted the seed of this weed as well as apples."

How did he plant his trees?

"He usually chose the most fertile spots, and he sometimes cleared the land and other times used clearings which the Indians had used. He saved the seeds at times, and sometimes put in bushels to the acre. After he had planted a nursery, he put a fence around it and he generally engaged some pioneer in the vicinity to look after it on condition that he should have a part of the trees. When his trees were grown, he sold them to such pioneers as could afford to pay for them and gave them to those that could not. He sometimes took notes, but he never asked a man to pay him any money that was due him, and he would take old clothes or anything else that he might need at the time in exchange for apple trees. He planted trees over fully a hundred square miles of territory, and he first came into Ohio in 1804. In 1806, he had two canoes on the Ohio river, and brought them to this state loaded with apple seeds. He did a great deal of good among the pioneers and he several times warned them on the approach of the Indians. He was treated well by the Indians as well as by the whites. And his orchards are still in existence all over this state. He believed that trees should be raised from the seed and not grafted, and he thought the apple was the most beautiful thing in fruit."

How did he die?

"He was in the western part of Indiana where he overdid himself in trying to reach one of his orchards which he was told the deer had entered and were eating the trees. Typhoid fever followed, and he died in Indiana at the age of

72. He felt his day was passing away with the march of civilization, and don't think he was impressed with the improvements of modern times. It was here in Mansfield that he took down the circuit-riding preacher, as has been published in the History of Richland County. The preacher was denouncing the sins of this life and the follies of dress. He was urging the men to be more simple in their ways and the women to tear the flowers from their bonnets, to sell their golden jewelry and give the proceeds to the Lord. At last he said, 'The primitive Christians have passed away; we have now no more saints on earth. Where, my hearers, will you now find the barefooted Christian traveling on his road to heaven?'

"At this, a loud voice was heard. The eyes of the crowd turned and, lying under a tree in the back of the square in his coffee-sack shirt and with his bare feet held high up in the air, Johnny Appleseed yelled out, 'Here, parson. Here is your primitive Christian.'"

During this talk, Dr. Bushnell showed me a sketch of Johnny Appleseed, which was drawn for a local novel of this region entitled "Phillip Seymour," and it is from this that the drawings in the present letter are made. The doctor says it is a good representation of this strangest of character.

Henry Stephens

John Chapman impressed two generations in the Bushnell family, William and his son, Martin, and the elder seemed to remember him with a clear, honest eye, long after he died. The Bushnells were respected in Mansfield, and their opinion probably went a long way to establishing Chapman as a real person, not just a cartoon character. They are also a link to another place the Bushnells and Appleseed were well known—Ashland County.

Chapter Thirteen

Horace S. Knapp's Frontispiece

Along with memories and stories, the earliest known picture of Johnny Appleseed originated in Richland, now Ashland, County. It was printed as a frontispiece in Horace S. Knapp's 1862 *History of Ashland County, Ohio*, and is supposedly based on the description that Rosella Rice wrote for the history. Evidence that suggests this might be true, even though nothing written confirms it, is his hat.

Rice described it in that publication as such:

> He hardly ever wore shoes, except in winter, but if traveling in the summer time and the rough roads hurt his feet, he would wear sandals and a big hat that he made himself out of pasteboard with one side very large and wide and bent down to keep the heat from his face.

She would also mention it in 1876 in *Arthur's Home Magazine*:

> His head covering was generally a pasteboard hat of his own making, with one broad side to it that he wore next the sunshine to protect his face. He wore it

with the wide side of the rim toward the sun. It was a very unsightly object, to be sure, and yet never one of us children ventured to laugh at it.

In 1888, Mansfield's Dr. William Bushnell, who said he knew John Chapman very well, was quoted in a newspaper article:

> As to Johnny Appleseed's hat he wore anything he could get that would cover his head, and he usually had a pasteboard visor, which he tied over his forehead to shield his eyes from the sun.

Figure 22. Horace S. Knapp's Frontiespiece in his 1862 History.

They were the only two to describe this kind of hat, although many others followed in many different stories, particularly the tin mush pot, a favorite to this day.

The picture in Knapp's 1862 history even shows hand-stitching around the brim of the hat that looks very much like a baseball cap. Since few people back then knew what baseball was, let alone the appropriate dress, subsequent reprinting of the Knapp Johnny Appleseed has that weird cap changed to something more recognizable, a floppy-brim field hat.

One other interesting detail is that Johnny Appleseed was often described, in words, as having a light beard—dark and hand trimmed. Knapp's picture shows no beard but there might be a little tuft of hair on the chin—hard to see. Rosella does not mention hairstyle, but another early biographer who claimed to know, Salathiel Coffinberry, wrote in 1871, "He never wore a full beard, but shaved all clean except a thin roach at the bottom of his throat."

The drawing also has the reputation, again not written down, of having been drawn by an Oberlin College student in the 1850s because he, or she, had known him personally, which may be questionable since he died a decade earlier, As it appears in the 1862 history, it is a well-done etching. What input the publisher, J. J. Lippincott Co., of Philadephia, had is unknown.

Only two other drawings appeared in the book, a rather generic log cabin and block house, both signed "A. Wilhelm." The Johnny Appleseed is larger, sharper but has no signature. This artist was never named.

Rosella was never known to illustrate anything, but there were plenty of young people in Ashland who attended Oberlin Academy, only 30 miles away. It could have been any son or daughter—of anyone.

Figure 23. Sketch with Johnny wearing a different hat.

It is tempting to tie the drawing to the Bushnell family, a large family found in both Richland and Ashland counties. Collins Bushnell, a cousin to Mansfield's William Bushnell, was a young man of 18 when he lived with the Horace Knapp family of Ashland in 1850. He was an orphan then, his parents dying young.

Knapp, then the editor of the Ashland *Union*, sold the paper in 1853 to pursue politics. Collins Bushnell bought it in 1855, but it returned to Knapp in 1857, when Bushnell, only 25, died. An early portrait of William Bushnell, a donation of a later generation, can be found in the Oberlin archives.

Knapp knew Rosella Rice well, through both the articles she wrote and her association with the county's educational system. He also solicited her opinion and description of Johnny Appleseed about the time (1857) she was writing about him in Roeliff Brinkerhoff's Mansfield *Herald* (see Chapter Ten).

In 1860, Knapp left the Ashland *Union* for the final time to write his history of Ashland County. His introduction illustrates his dedication to getting it right, not just turning it over to people's shining memories of ancestors:

> An accurate history of the events sought to be given derives more importance from the fact that several writers of the purely "sensation" stamp have so caricatured, in publications they have made, certain prominent incidents connected with the early settlement of the territory now forms the county, that truth and falsehood have been utterly confounded. Had the effort to vindicate the truth of history against the assaults of mere romancers been much longer delayed, the period would soon, in the course of nature, have forever passed....

He thanks a lot of local people, including Rosella, but his own honesty and impatience is displayed in taking a swipe at the recalcitrant federal post office department and various local churches who ignored his inquiries. Because of this, he seems like a man who would run a picture of Johnny Appleseed only if people who knew him agreed to its accuracy.

Afterword

John Chapman was a living, breathing person. Over the years too much fantasy about his life has been mixed in and shaken well with too little facts to produce the legend that became Johnny Appleseed. The problem is not so much that too little has been written about him but that too much has been written—layer after layer, generation after generation, fantasy after fantasy.

To find the truest picture of the man, I looked for the people who knew him, who met him, and remembered him as accurately as they could. These were the people who were also given the opportunity, or seized it themselves, to put their memories in writing, well preserved for future readers.

These were the people found in the same place where the legends started to branch off— Richland County, Ohio. My purpose is to present the lost stories and the best storytellers in order to discern the truth. Sometimes old, stale history yields new, fresh information to those with the patience to look, like Dwight Wesley Garber, whose search after the truth and knowledge of local history inspired this book.

Although both he and I discovered that a lot of the Johnny Appleseed stories were quite obviously fiction, I found them filled with bits and pieces of fact from authors who were alive when they happened. By laying these stories side by side with other such stories, I looked for what was the same and what was different and compared them to what else has survived as provable fact in search of what was true.

I looked at the authors and what they hoped to accomplish—at Rosella Rice's stories to judge whether a young girl looking over her mother's shoulder at a ragged but fascinating "old" man was telling the truth.

In the end, I discovered an interesting whole rather than layers of stale stories told and retold and changed. By reading some fresh good information straight, if not from Heaven, then from Johnny's real, and truthful, friends.

Acknowledgments

First of all, I would like to thank Dwight Wesley Garber, who died on October 29, 1983. He is buried next to his wife, Vera, in LaGrange, Oregon, where she had family. They lived many of their last years in Stockton, California, to be near their daughter, the late Connie Cullen.

Garber was born on April 26, 1896, in Butler, Ohio, and he never forgot that Ohio was the home of his birth. Much of his historical research began there and continued with new concentration after his retirement from the Navy and return to Richland County. His skill and persistence made this book possible.

I also wish to thank two historians to whom Garber was a mentor, Robert A. Carter of Mansfield and Theresa M. Flaherty, who is spending her and her husband's retirement traveling across the country in a motorhome, and another historian, Michael C. Cullen, of Pensacola, Florida, to whom Garber was grandfather. All inherited Garber's love of the past and agreed the immense amount of work put into his manuscript should not be lost.

Their story may be found in *Water-Powered Mills of Richland County* by Robert A. Carter and Michael C. Cullen, edited by Theresa Marie Flaherty, and published by Turas Publishing in 2016.

I am also grateful to the late Richland County historian and genealogist, Mary Jane Henney of Mansfield, who among hundreds of her other valuable projects for the Ohio Genealogical Society was fascinated by the Perrysville author, Rosella Rice. She contacted many descendants, found her articles and wrote the book, *Rosella Rice* (1827-1888), which is available by mail through the Ashland County Chapter of the Ohio Genealogical Society, P.O. Box 681 Ashland, Ohio 44805-0681, *ashlandgenealogy.org*. It includes some Johnny Appleseed information.

Many of the original Rice family records as well as Rosella's manuscripts have been donated to the Butler-Clear Fork Valley Historical Society by James Beveridge of Butler, a great-great-grandson of Rosella's half-sister, Ida Rice Wilson. Contact the society at *butlermuseumoh.webs.com*. Other Garber material, including that on Rosella Rice and her cousin, Mary O. Eddy, may be found at the museum.

Helping Henney in the 1990s with the Rice project was longtime Johnny Appleseed scholar William Ellery Jones of Cincinnati, who authored an update on *Johnny Appleseed, a Voice in the Wilderness* published by the Swedenborg Foundation, and also was the motivating force behind the Johnny Appleseed Heritage Center and Outdoor Historical Drama and the state-supported Johnny Appleseed Historic Byway in Richland and Ashland counties. He also was founder and president for many years of the Greentown Preservation Association of Ashland County to save the Delaware Indian village site. The book would not be possible without Jones' continual encouragement and contributions.

And thank you to all the descendants, historians, authors, libraries, and museums of Richland and Ashland counties that lent information on a strange but beloved man named Johnny Appleseed. This area understandably is full of that information—for those who are willing to look.

Other Richland County Researchers

These are more people from either Richland and Ashland counties, or both, who over the years became obsessed with Johnny Appleseed. They may have had other historic interests but Johnny Appleseed was primary. They became "experts." They may have written and published a book or books on him.

Some local historians build their entire project on other people's research. Others may act, at least at first, as if they are starting from scratch, as if no one else ever found anything. I like to think that if persistent enough, both will improve the research, making new discoveries and disproving old. Those who blindly depend on others are doomed to continue the same mistakes. Those who start without knowing what has already been done are doomed to a lot of unnecessary work.

Those who plan to research Johnny Appleseed should know what these people knew. Much can be learned about him in Richland and Ashland counties.

Anna Long Onstott (1869-1944)

Raised in Mansfield, she came rather late to historical research of Appleseed but accomplished quite a lot around the state just by talking—to his relatives, to other researchers, to schoolchildren, to various social groups, to politicians, and to journalists, both local and national. The wife of a Methodist minister, the Reverend Daniel Onstott, she traveled with him and searched for various things that interested her. She never got around to writing a book about Appleseed but did write several articles for church publications. She organized official commemorative days. She tracked down a Bible that was said to belong to Appleseed and descended in the family of his half sister Persis Chapman Broom Snow. That Bible was donated to the Johnny Appleseed Center at Urbana University in Ohio.

At some point she got copies of a 1925 Dix family letter and a 1776 letter from Johnny's mother via a great-granddaughter, Bertha B. Dix, who then lived in Michigan. The contents of the letter have been widely circulated and can be found in almost every biography, but the location of the original is a mystery.

William J. Duff (1872-1950)

He was born in Ashland, Ohio, and spent most of his adult life in newspapers, among them the Mansfield *News* for about eight years and the Mansfield *Shield* for three. He returned to Ashland and edited the Ashland *Times-Gazette* until 1926. He did love to write, both fiction and non-fiction, and churned out a history column and a radio show. He also loved research, and various newspaper stories say he had 160 scrapbooks and millions of clippings in his house. The author of several books, including the 1932 three-volume set of *The History of North Central Ohio*, he was particularly fond of Johnny Appleseed and credited with spreading his fame at least throughout the state. In 1915 he solicited copper pennies and stone boulders from area schoolchildren, and a monument was erected in Ashland. Duff's columns may be found in microfilmed Ashland newspapers and a small portion of his scrapbook and clippings collection is in the Ashland County Historical Society museum.

H. Kenneth Dirlam (1881-1970)

A Mansfield native, he was a banker but also produced and distributed thousands of books because he wanted to inspire interest in local history. The first was *A Gatherer and Planter of Appleseeds*, where he gathered, for the convenience of his readers, much of the facts of Johnny Appleseed's life as well as some stories that had taken root in local families. He proudly included in this slim book's many editions the thousands of requests for copies from schools and libraries and others. He was an enthusiastic marketer and took advantage of the interest in Johnny Appleseed by post-World War II baby-boomers and the renewed interest in the 1950s and 1960s, prompted in part by the 1948 Disney animated feature and music and Robert Price's 1954 book. Mansfield had, or would soon have, a Johnny Appleseed school, shopping center, a Boy Scout council, and even a hotel cafeteria. Dirlam lectured widely and showed up with other Appleseed devotees, like Price, at many dedications. He later published a longer *Bits of History* book that included many local subjects but started with Johnny Appleseed. Neither book is in print, but many have been available on the secondary market.

D. W. Garber's acknowledgements from his 50-year-old manuscript on Johnny Appleseed are included next, simply because the recipients deserve it. Many are now deceased, but the passing along of this information and the preservation of these comments are vital to Garber's project. Not all their contributions survived into this book; however, naming them might provide clues to further research into a myriad of local subjects.

Peggy Welch Mershon

Dwight Wesley Garber

Unpublished Acknowledgments in 1972

Acknowledgments long overdue are gladly given to Rosella Rice and Andrew [*later found to be Salathiel*] Coffinberry for their "lost contributions" to the story of Johnny Appleseed.

The kindness of the following members of the Rice family, each of whom permitted the use of material of great interest, is gratefully acknowledged: Mr. and Mrs. Francis Stahl, Russell Stahl, James Culler, Mrs. Lucille Craig, Mrs. A.J. Beveridge and Mrs. Eugene Beck.

Special thanks are due Dr. Mary O. Eddy, a descendant of the pioneer Coulter family (of Perrysville) and doubly related to Rosella Rice, for personal reminiscences of Rosella, for Rosella Rice manuscripts and for a family album containing the Coulter-Rice pictures used as illustration.

Personal interviews with Harmon Kochheiser, John E. Cowan, Henry B. Odell, Georgiana (Mrs. Charles) W. Fuchs and Leora Kanaga provided interesting items of information.

Outstanding has been the generosity of Robert A. Carter, who made available his collection of Watson family documents and gave the author two letters written by Amariah Watson Jr., concerning his services in the War of 1812.

Robert G. Hayman, Kenneth O. Dudley, Ernest J. Wessen, and Nellie (Mrs. S.G.) Raber have added materially to the store of information. Norman L. Wolfe and Ray H. Priest permitted the use of old account books which contribute to the story of Johnny Appleseed and his activities.

Frank L. Crone, a genealogist of note with a lifetime interest in Mohican history, gave the benefit of his research into the history of the Frontier Rangers.

Thanks go to the staff of the Western Reserve Historical Society Library for patient assistance and for permission to use the earliest known issue of The *Richland Jeffersonian* containing a Gottfried story; and to the Ohio Historical Society Library and the Mansfield Public Library for many kindnesses. Also the Ohio State Library for permission to reproduce the three petitions sent to Gov. Return J. Meigs by the settlers in Richland County; the Library of Congress for a copy of the *Richland Herald* and *Democratic Advertiser,* the predecessor of the *Richland Jeffersonian.*

Clarifying information concerning the Swedenborgian doctrine was generously provided by Tomas [sic] H. Spiers, executive secretary of the Swedenborg Foundation, and the Rev. Leslie Marshall, formerly the editor of the Swedenborg Press.

Through correspondence Etta Gilkison Mitchell, a granddaughter of John C. Gilkison, gave personal and family recollections.

Acknowledgment is also made to the following for permission to quote from books they published: Doubleday and Co., *The Tree Book* by Julia Ellen Rogers; the public library of Fort Wayne an Allen County, Ind.; Robert C. Harris' *Johnny*

Appleseed Source Book; and Little, Brown and Co., Benard DeVoto's *Forays and Rebuttals,* quoted by permission of Mrs. Bernard DeVoto, owner of the copyright.

Dr. Robert Price, the foremost authority of the life of Johnny Appleseed, devoted many hours to reading the manuscript and kindly suggested improvements in the organization and use of the material.

Thanks inadequately express the deep obligation to Dr. and Mrs. Arthur J. Cullen for critical advice; Dr. Ruth Marie Faurot for valuable editorial assistance; and Mrs. Marilyn G. Hood, editor of special publications for the Ohio Historical Society, for reading the manuscript and offering constructive comments. Also Mrs. Theresa M. Flaherty, an efficient secretary and an admirer of Johnny Appleseed, for typing the manuscript.

And last, but foremost in appreciation, the recognition due my wife, Vera S. Garber, for her consistently patient and good-natured encouragement, without which the project would never have been completed.

D. W. Garber

The Author
Peggy Welch Mershon

A graduate in journalism from Kent State University, Peggy Mershon has lived in the Mansfield, Ohio, area since 1974 and started as a reporter and editor for the *News Journal* in 1978. She also wrote weekly columns for this newspaper on genealogy, antiques, and history. She was the editor of the weekly Bellville, Ohio, *Star* for several years. She has been a member of the Ohio Genealogical Society, the Richland County Genealogical Society, the Bellville-Jefferson Township Historical Society, the Greentown Preservation Association and the Butler-Clear Fork Valley Historical Society. She also served as curator of the Butler historical museum and was instrumental in acquiring its Rosella Rice collections.

She was chosen by the family and friends of the late Dwight Wesley Garber of Richland County to review the material and unfinished manuscript in his project on Johnny Appleseed that he had collected and worked on from 1948 through the early 1970s. Peggy was asked to find a story in the material that would be uniquely hers. After her thorough review and many hours of additional research, Peggy has captured the essence of John Chapman, the man, and confirmed his rightful place as an historical figure – not a legend.

www.ingramcontent.com/pod-product-compliance
Lightning Source LLC
Chambersburg PA
CBHW070600010526
44118CB00012B/1396